Online Success: 7 Steps to a Powerful Internet Presence

What small organizations, entrepreneurs, freelancers, writers, and business owners need to know about how to build an effective online presence.

To a talented artist! Much success!

Beth Gramling Sanders

Printed in the United States of America First Printing, 2018
ISBN 978-0-692-88536-9

Beth G. Sanders
P.O. Box 381861
Germantown, TN 38183-1861

BethGSanders.com

Cover design by Beth G. Sanders

Book design and production by Beth G. Sanders

Author photograph by Beth G. Sanders
(Yes, I did use a selfie for my book.)

Acknowledgements

Thanks to our beloved children, daughters Elizabeth Sanders and Sara Ann Sanderlin, and son-in-law Ethan Sanderlin. They have endured my texting and talking ad nauseum about this book and have provided valuable encouragement through the process.

To my dear friends who believed me when I said I'm writing a book, and my amazing consulting clients who have inspired this book and who make my work so enjoyable.

The encouragement and support of my advisory committee, Barbara Price, Eva Lang, and Jo Ellen Druelinger have helped convince me I could write a book and empowered me to finish. Longtime print nerd friend Kellee LaVars gifted me with her publishing expertise to help me trek through unfamiliar ground. To Adobe InDesign, my sometime nemesis, we've been together since you were born. I'm so glad I dumped PageMaker and Quark XPress for you all those years ago. It's been fun (Yes, I know it's a piece of software. Indulge me).

My Daddy was the first person to tell me I have a talent for writing and encouraged me by asking me to edit his orthodontic journal articles and submitting and publishing them with my edits. If there are books in Heaven, he'll be reading this one even though he never lived to have an email address. He was a lifelong learner and inspired me to be as well. And I'm sure he's rejoicing that I found something to do with my life that does not involve algebra.

I'm grateful for God's grace and presence in my life, my extended family, oaky-buttery chardonnays, the Messengers Sunday School class, New York City in the snow, Simon and Garfunkel, and

for group texts with my daughters.

More than anything, I'm grateful for Jim, my husband of 31 years, who, as editor of this book, reviewed about 95,000 revisions and provided insight, feedback and suggestions that have made this book 300 percent* better than it was when I put it in his hands.

*This figure is, at best, a wild guess, because I don't do numbers. But Jim helped a lot.

Dedication

This book is dedicated to the memory of my nephew, my dude, Sam VanScoy, who left this world far too early.

I chose this photo because it perfectly represents his sense of fun and humor. That wry smile you see is because, once again, he got over on his crazy old aunt, Dodo (aka me). He was quite pleased with himself.

We were at dinner at a nice restaurant in Jonesboro, and I admired his new sportcoat and asked him to smile for a photo. I should have known he was all too cooperative. At the last moment he purposely turned his head and this photo is the result.

I miss him like crazy and think about him every day. I miss his smartass wit, I miss him calling me *Grandmother* in Spanish (Abuela) just in case I ever forgot I'm not young anymore. My sister's baby boy, my geek buddy, protector of coveted silent auction items (ask me sometime about my Roy Halladay-autographed baseball), hipster foodie, my World Series buddy, *mi sobrino,* I love you. I miss you.

I will see you again someday.

Contents

Introduction

As a web designer, social media coach and tech consultant, I teach my clients how to use social media and the internet to build business relationships and tell their stories online. I build websites for them that anchor their online presence and give them a professional first impression, and coach them on how to integrate social media, email marketing, and blogging into their web strategy. The material in this book is derived from hours of client consulting over the past 11 years.

I started using social media around 2006, when it was in its infancy. The only users who were seriously active were college kids on Facebook and the geek/early adopter crowd. It's hard to believe that in those days you would find it nearly impossible to convince a business owner or leader of an organization that social media was a worthwhile endeavor. They didn't understand it and they were afraid of it. Specifically, the idea that you have people talking about you online and you can't control the ideas being expressed was scary and foreign. For conventional marketing executives and business owners, that was a frightening thought, one nearly no one was willing to entertain.

Social media continued to grow on its own, with many conventional marketers ignoring it, often calling it a fad. In 2009, Twitter reached what CNBC calls its defining moment.[1] On January 15, Captain Chesley B. "Sully" Sullenberger III landed US Airways Flight 1549 in the Hudson River after the plane was crippled by a bird strike. Sullenberger's quick decision and cool head saved hundreds of lives and the incident was referred to as *The Miracle on the Hudson*. On that day there were dozens of Twitter users in the area and their tweets, photographs, and videos broke the news 15 minutes before the major news outlets knew what had happened.[2]

The media world was forever changed. For the first time, news was broken by a regular citizen, not CNN, ABC, NBC, CBS, or the other major television networks. You might say that Twitter — and social media — came of age that day.

The rise of social media had a ripple effect throughout the internet. Experts began to talk about Web 2.0, which simply meant the new, interactive internet. Users began to expect two-way communication and businesses scrambled to set up blogs on their websites to encourage comments and feedback.

As I write this today, it's hard to remember a time when two-way communication wasn't a part of internet life. Even the skeptics have been convinced; interactivity is here to stay, and with it a plethora of online services that can help us reach our audience effectively and build online relationships and thought leadership.

To compete in today's online-focused world, we must make use of the tools that make sense for our business. The web is simply one of many communication channels that allow us to build relationships with our audience that inspire loyalty and engagement. The possibilities are endless, and the purpose of this book is to help you find your way and use the internet and social media as effective business tools.

Although the interactive web has been around for years, not everyone jumped on board in the beginning. Marketers didn't want to change their approach from *outbound marketing,* that is, promotions that are pushed to the customer, such as television and radio advertising, direct mail, brochures, newspaper and magazine advertising and other approaches that involve the advertiser sending their message to their customers.

Web interactivity brought with it the concept of *inbound marketing,* which attracts the customer and pulls them in. Inbound marketing may mean you add a blog to your website or become active on social media sites where your audience is active. Your efforts are best focused on content that solves the readers' problems and makes them want to read more.

When you post on your blog on social media platforms, you have an opportunity to interact with your customers, hear their feedback, and reply to them. You're not posting sales copy; your content is aimed toward solving the problems that keep your customers awake at night. They are attracted to you because you help them and you talk to them. You forge relationships and loyalty that keep them coming back.

The best thing you can do for your business — and one of the most difficult — is to keep your customers foremost in your mind as you build your online presence. Every decision you make must be weighed by that measure.

Step 1

Know Your Audience

Y ou've read the introduction and you are ready to go. Buy the domain, look for images, write copy … WAIT. We've just discussed the most important attitude you can cultivate in yourself and your staff: customer focus. This is the ability to put yourself in your customer's shoes and focus on their wishes and needs rather than your own. How do you do that if you don't know them?

You can't unless you work at it. If you already have an established customer base, excellent. You have built-in models to consider and commit to memory.

Because it's so difficult for most of us to put aside our own preferences, likes, and dislikes, most marketing experts recommend using an *avatar* or *persona*. The two words mean essentially the same thing in this context. It's a way of visualizing your target market as individuals. You'll deep dive into your ideal customer — who they are, their likes and dislikes, their needs, their wants, and struggles. What's their lifestyle? Are they urban dwellers or suburbanites, or do they live in a rural area? What's their income level?

If you have a team, brainstorm your avatar as a group. You can build more than one avatar. Imagine them one at a time and get down to details. When you finish, you have a picture of at least one of your typical customers. Once you know what makes them tick, you're in a better position to respond to their needs.

Asparagus and Your Avatar

I hate asparagus. I hate it so much I won't even eat it wrapped in bacon. I know it's a delicacy, it's pretty and it's expensive, but I cannot stand it.

I also hate duck. I've eaten it prepared by a gourmet cook, bathed in a delicious sauce, and in a spicy gumbo I made myself. Still, duck = yuck. Finally, at the risk of losing my Southerner card, I cannot stand potato salad. I love potatoes, but mix them up with mayonnaise, serve them cold and, no thank you.

I'll bet you have at least three food yucks as well. Imagine you're invited to an elegant dinner party at a friend's home. You sit down to an exquisite table, and the host proudly tells you he's prepared his favorite meal just for you. There's a lovely glass of wine, candlelight, and on the fine china in front of you is a meal consisting of your equivalent of my duck, asparagus and potato salad.

You've made the trip to your friend's house and you're starving, but there is nothing on the plate in front of you that you can eat. It's obvious he has spent hours preparing the meal and the setting, so you appreciate the effort, politely make awkward conversation, push the vile mess around your plate, and leave hungry.

The host's mistake was preparing *his* favorite meal. He didn't ask for your preferences, he built an evening

> If you miss on customer insight and focus, your marketing efforts will fail no matter what you do.

around his own personal tastes. While it might have made a lovely magazine feature, the dinner party failed miserably and the guest went home hungry.

What does disgusting food have to do with marketing? I relate this hypothetical story to shed light on one of the most difficult mind shifts we must make as we market our business: to put aside our own preferences, likes, and dislikes to serve our customers. There's nearly always a difference in what we like and what appeals to our customers. Given the choice, most of us would say, "Yes, of course I'd rather please my potential customers." But do we mean it?

It's a good idea to get advice from a professional about what *converts*, or sells, the best. This will probably be different from what you would have chosen. If budget allows, assemble a *focus group*, a group of individuals who provide candid feedback. You'll almost always be surprised at the difference between internal preferences and those of focus groups. At the very least, ask a few customers. If there's disagreement, always decide in favor of the customer.

Television's popular Property Brothers star in a program that features a family who wants to sell their house and buy a more suitable property. The show centers around the search for a new home and suggested renovations to their existing home to facilitate a faster and more profitable sale. I'm tempted to yell at the TV screen when homeowners resist expert advice about what buyers want and balk at the proposed changes to their home in favor of their own preferences. Please yourself and you'll get to keep your house. Delight potential buyers with a clean, fresh home that appeals to them and you'll soon be loading the moving van.

If you miss on customer insight and focus, your marketing efforts will fail no matter what you do. The glossiest brochure, coolest website, and smartest email marketing program will fall flat if it's focused on you rather than your target customer. This is why I mentioned the avatar in the introduction to this chapter. It's a valuable exercise to help you get into the mind of your potential customers or clients.

Let's say I've opened a cafe in an urban up-and-coming neighborhood full of young families. They range in age from 30 to 40 years old, dual-income couples, college educated, with combined incomes between $50,000 and $80,000. Most are politically left-leaning, concerned about the environment, good public schools for their kids, and quality daycare. They value healthy eating, locally-sourced foods and seek out local businesses to patronize. Time is always in short supply, so they prioritize carefully.

Now that you know who your audience is, you can meet their needs. Prices must be affordable, so you concentrate on simple foods with ingredients you can buy fresh from local farmers. Perhaps you provide a recycling bin and use only green products. Your decor and ambiance communicate a safe, comfortable place for children and families that is colorful and fun. Service is friendly and personal and you get to know your customers by name.

You can see how this understanding of the customer base influences the shape of the business — everything from the decor to the menu. Even though this is a fictional business, the owners have set the stage for customer loyalty, repeat business, and have made success a likely prediction.

My husband and I once ate at an excellent restaurant with a lovely, elegant interior. We enjoyed a delightful evening with delicious food and wine and impeccable service. I was disappointed but not surprised when I heard they had closed after only a few months. They did everything right — but apparently skipped the avatar exercise. They were far too upscale and formal for their young, trendy, middle-income neighborhood full of lively bars and more casual eateries.

Here's a template to help you build your own avatar. You can add to it as needed.

- Age Group
- Socioeconomic factors: Income, expenses
- Family composition: Empty nesters, young children, teenagers, caring for elderly relatives
- Style preferences: Clothing, cars, home decor
- Interests: Hobbies, pastimes, sports, travel
- Habits: Do they go out or stay in? Do they entertain friends at home or meet up at a bar or restaurant? Are they frugal or do they splurge on luxury goods?
- Concerns: Local issues, crime, education
- Political leaning

This is not by any means an exhaustive list, but I hope it will get your started in the right direction. Answer these questions about your market and you'll be better able to meet their needs. Let your avatar shape both how you conduct your business and how you market. Remember, it's not about you, it's about *them*.

Step 2

Choose Your Keywords

Now that you've defined your avatar(s), the next step is what I believe to be the foundation of your online strategy — your keywords. If you've heard of keywords, it's likely in the context of *search engine optimization* (SEO), the practice of *organically* (without paying) increasing a website's visibility in search results. I'd like to suggest that your entire online strategy be established around these words. Think about these words carefully and devote plenty of time to this exercise.

Several years ago, I thought I had done an excellent job with keywords. I have a friend and colleague who is an SEO expert and we agreed to barter services; she would teach me about SEO and I would help with her WordPress website. As I showed her my website, I hoped she would be impressed. She did like the design, but she questioned me on my title, *digital communications consultant.* I must have looked like a deer in the headlights when she asked how many of my potential clients I thought would search for the term *digital communications consultant*. I'd been using a term that made sense to me, but not to the people I wanted to reach. I had ignored my audience. I've since become a social media consultant, writer, and WordPress web designer, which I think are far more accessible.

Search terms, or keywords, are how many of your readers will find you online, so decide carefully which words or phrases will draw the best traffic. Don't do what I did — instead of using words that sound good to you, ask yourself what words a regular person who needs your services would use to find you online. Or better yet, ask your customers.

Let's brainstorm. Think of 10 to 15 keywords that communicate your *unique selling proposition* (USP), or what sets you apart from your competition. They can also be short phrases. Keywords aren't just for search engines, they are for everything you do online. Keep them in mind when you're building your social media posts, blog posts, and in your email marketing. Remember, keywords are words that regular people will use to search for you online. They are not industry jargon words.

Long-Tail Keywords

Wordtracker.com describes long-tail keywords like this:
> Long-tail keywords are those three- and four-keyword phrases which are very, very specific to whatever you are selling. You see, whenever a customer uses a highly specific search phrase, they tend to be looking for exactly what they are actually going to buy. In virtual-

ly every case, such very specific searches are far more
likely to convert to sales than general generic searches
that tend to be geared more toward the type of re-
search that consumers typically do prior to making a
buying decision.[3]

While long-tail keywords may bring less traffic or fewer prospects, the prospects are generally better qualified. If I search for *TV,* I will get thousands of results; if I enter

> I'd like to suggest that your entire online strategy be established around your keywords.

BrandX 70" TV, my search will return results much more closely aligned with what I'm looking for. In addition, long-tail keywords generally have less competition. Imagine trying to rank for a general term like *TV.* Forget organic traffic — you'd have to pay enormous advertising dollars to get on the first page of results for a keyword this popular. Using the long-tail keyword *BrandX 70" TV* would cost much less and bring much more traffic related to your product.

We'll talk more in later chapters about how to incorporate and consider your keywords in your online marketing. When you think about these words, remember your audience may not be educated about what you do. Ask friends, relatives, or better yet, customers, how they would search for you. Your keywords should reflect what you want to be found for online, so choose them carefully. For example, I teach social media, online networking, and I build WordPress websites so I use all of these keywords. This exercise will drive everything we do throughout this book, so invest the time and choose the right keywords and phrases.

There are tools to help you find keywords that relate to your content; a simple Google search for keyword tools will return enough results to keep you busy on a rainy weekend. Most allow you to download them in spreadsheet form.

Time spent thinking about your keywords will not be wasted; it will help you develop a cohesive and effective online presence.

Step 3

Your Website

Too many organizations underestimate the importance of an effective website. Your website is your digital front door. It may be the only thing some potential customers see, and it may be their first impression of your brand.

My husband and I love a nice dinner out. When we travel, we always look for an excellent restaurant for a special dinner date. Often we know little to nothing about the cities we visit, so I begin my research with a Google search: *Best restaurant in <city>*. From there I look at reviews on various sites, feature articles about the restaurant, and social media posts, but I never fail to visit their website.

Just like the exterior of a building, most of us can size up a restaurant from their website in a few seconds. Is it casual, upscale, formal, family friendly? Will your ice water be served in a Mason jar or a footed crystal goblet? Is it trendy or classic, French, Italian, or New American? Will the waiter laugh if you ask for a wine list? You can probably figure out most of this information by a glance at the front door, or from the restaurant's website.

Have you thought about what your website says about your business? Does it honestly and accurately represent your USP? Is it up to date? How does it perform on mobile devices? A website that looks like it was designed in the 1990s and isn't mobile friendly is like a physical entrance with chipping paint, broken glass, and a rat or two guarding the door.

> ... if you do not plan to make your website mobile friendly, just don't bother.

If you already have a great website, I hope this chapter will help you evaluate it to see if there's anything you've missed. Not too long ago I went to the website of a local restaurant, a lovely site. After I looked at the menu and determined it sounded appetizing, I checked for the location. Nowhere on the restaurant's website could I find the address. I finally had to call them to ask where they are located, which wasted their time on a busy night and complicated my user experience.

We'll talk about the elements your website cannot and should not live without. I want to be very clear that if you do not plan to make your website mobile friendly, just don't bother. According to Marketing Land, " ... roughly 56 percent of consumer traffic to the leading U.S. websites is now from mobile devices."[4] What this means for online businesses is that, no matter how amazing your site looks on a computer screen, if it doesn't adapt to smaller screen sizes, you're going to lose most users.

Website Structure

To better understand how websites are put together, bear with me for a bit of technical explanation. The language of the internet is HTML, which stands for *hypertext markup language.* What this means is that any content to be displayed on a web page must be translated into HTML. If you have a Microsoft Word document that you want to be a web page, it must be reformatted into HTML.

There is a hierarchy of content in HTML. There are six levels of headings, <H1> through <H6>, descending in importance. In HTML, all elements are structured using tags. An HTML tag is enclosed in angle brackets. The text to appear on the page must be enclosed between an open tag <> and a close tag </>.

Your <H1> tag is the most important one on the page; it's the one that search engines look for first. The <H1> should contain at least one keyword and it must give the reader an idea of what the page is about. You should have only one <H1> heading on a page and it must be at the top of the page. Other headings should follow, so that <H2> is the next most important, <H3> comes under <H2>, and so forth.

Regular body text will be defined by the paragraph, or <p> tag. As with the headings, you'll need to close the tag </p>. The only exception to the close tag rule is that an image <img> has no close tag. There are other tags such as bullet lists, numbered lists, and blockquotes, but what you need to know to optimize your pages for search engines is the hierarchy of the heading tags. Most popular content management systems will provide a WSIWYG (*what you see is what you get*) interface, so you won't have to remember the tags.

Header

The header is the very top of the site and generally contains your logo, site name, site title and navigation. A general web convention is that a click on the header logo takes you back to the home page. Your header may be a contrasting color, or it may be laid over an image and be transparent. Some modern websites don't have a visible header, but will still have the following elements.

Logo/Site Name — Your logo must be displayed large enough to read any text, but not so large as to dominate the page. If you don't have a logo, use your name. Add your name as text; don't put it in an image if you can avoid it. Search engines cannot pick up text in an image, so don't waste the SEO opportunity. Remember, Google looks first for the <H1> heading. If your <H1> is nonexistent because you've used an image to represent it, you make it more difficult for Google to find and index your site. Help Google find your site by keeping your <H1> as regular text or, at the very least, add your business name in *alt text,* a word or phrase inserted as an attribute on an image.

Site Title — Your site title is shown in the browser tab when a user is on your site. The browser tab at the top will display the name of your site (*YourSite.com*) and generally a divider and a keyword or phrase you designate. For example, *YourSite | Best Widget Maker.*

Navigation — Your site navigation is the menu, generally at the top: the list of pages, categories, or posts that make up your website and link to the respective pages. The font should be readable. Use one-word links in your menu wherever possible to avoid a line break on smaller screens. You may also have subpages that make up a dropdown list, such as a blog with its categories. The dropdown list will only appear when the user hovers on the top-level item. On a mobile device, the menu will be represented by an icon that resembles a hamburger (if you think really hard about it), with three stacked horizontal lines. This hamburger menu is becoming increasingly popular on desktop websites as well.

Other Header Elements

Social Follow Buttons — You may add these in the header, where they'll be easily seen. They also work well in the footer, as most interested viewers will see them when they scroll down. In the header, you'll often see them on the upper right side as studies have shown this part of the page gets more views.

Site Search — Especially if you write about more than one topic, or if you have a lot of content, a search form will help your users find the content they are looking for. For an e-commerce site you definitely need a search form to help the customer find a specific product.

Contact Information — Depending on the nature of your business you may want to add a telephone number in the header. If you're a local business, such as a restaurant or other service, or have a toll-free number that customers use regularly, this can work well. Make the phone number a live link so that mobile users can easily place a call.

Email Capture Form — You may choose to put your email capture form in the header; usually at the top right. It's a smart placement, as that's where our eyes naturally travel when the page loads.

Main Content Section

This is the meat of the site, where your main copy and images live. It can be full width or include a sidebar. Many sites use a full-width home page and a sidebar layout on the inside pages; make your own decision based on your content. It should be easy to read and use a font that is large enough to be easily seen.

Most websites use *sans-serif* fonts (such as Arial, Verdana, or Helvetica) for text because it is easier to read on screen. A sans-serif font has no strokes or lines at the ends. Times New Roman and Garamond are examples of *serif* fonts. While serif fonts are generally easier to read in print, the opposite is generally thought to be true on the web — for this reason, most modern websites use sans-serif fonts for body copy.

Whatever font you choose, be sure it has enough contrast with the background that it does not create an obstacle for the reader. Use a dark color on a light background for best readability, and make your text large enough to be read easily.

Sidebar

The sidebar is just what it sounds like; a bar or column on the right or left side that contains extra information that doesn't go in the main section. Here you can include your social follow buttons, any offers you have, an email capture form and any other links that are important. You can also include a social media feed if you'd like, which will show your tweets, Instagram photos or Facebook posts.

You'll notice most modern websites don't have sidebars on the home page; the current trend is toward full-width sites and many sites don't have sidebars even on the inner pages. On a mobile device, the sidebar will generally drop down below the rest of the content, making it significantly less visible.

Footer

The footer appears at the bottom of each page and contains information you wish to be seen sitewide. It may contain a contact form, social media follow buttons, or other extras. It should always include your business name, address, phone, and copyright date.

Content Management Systems (CMS)

Unless you're a web developer, most business owners hire a professional to design and build their websites. This can get expensive and become troublesome if you update your website regularly. For that reason, I recommend a *content management system* (CMS) like WordPress.

A CMS allows you to edit and update your own website, and, if you are so inclined, you can even design it yourself. It will be beneficial to know a bit of HTML and the language that gives HTML its style, *CSS,* which stands for *Cascading Style Sheets.* While HTML provides the structure of the page, CSS controls the presentation, or look of the page. I like to compare it to a house: if HTML is the walls, floors, ceilings, doors, and windows, CSS is the wallpaper, carpet, pictures on the walls, and paint. In brief, good HTML makes it stand strong, good CSS makes it beautiful.

WordPress: Why it's the Best Solution

There are many considerations as you begin to design your website. Many large corporations' websites are designed and developed by high-end agencies at costs that start in the five-figure range. These companies may have entire teams who update and maintain their websites.

Those who lack the budget required for agency work would do well to consider options that allow small businesses or individuals to design and edit their own sites, such as a CMS.

WordPress is the most popular CMS by far. Approximately 28.9 percent of the entire internet runs on WordPress, which is a total of nearly 16 million sites.[5]

Today even large corporations are using CMS solutions like WordPress to power their websites and blogs. Ford Motor Company, The Walt Disney Company, and *The New York Times* are examples. The fact that WordPress is ideal for both high-profile, high-traffic sites, and small businesses demonstrates its flexibility and scalability.

Here are a few reasons I'm partial to Wordpress.

- The large market share. More than one in four of all websites are built on WordPress. With more than 16 million sites, that's a large piece of the market. What this means for the user is that there is an enormous community of WordPress users and readily-available support for nearly any issue you might encounter.
- WordPress is excellent for SEO straight out of the box. The organization of content into categories and the way WordPress presents your content helps you get found in search engines.
- WordPress lets you control your own website. For most of my website clients, before I turn over the site to them, I provide a one-hour orientation session. That's generally enough to get them comfortable with updating and adding content to their site. Rather than hiring a developer

to fix a typo or make copy changes, you can do those yourself. Lest you think I'm suggesting you take work away from web developers, rest assured that copy changes are not the sort of work that web developers like to do.

- You can easily add additional functionality to your site without hiring a programmer.

WordPress comes out of the box with everything you need for an excellent basic website, but most of us need features beyond the basic. For this you will go to *plugins,* pieces of software you add to your WordPress installation. For example, Yoast SEO is arguably the leading search engine optimization plugin. There's no real magic, but the plugin prompts you to add keywords, descriptions and lets you know how well you've optimized your post or page for search engines. There are also plugins for events lists, polls, social media integration, building membership sites, events calendars, and security.

Don't lose valuable traffic from your blog— keep it on the same domain as your website.

Some plugins come with widgets. Widgets allow you to drag and drop elements into designated areas. Some users get confused by widgets, as some widgets are plugins, some are not. Some plugins are widgets, and some are not. Clear as mud? Don't worry, you'll catch on once you start using WordPress regularly; and even if you don't it won't stop you from using WordPress well.

I use a plugin on my personal blog that places my Instagram feed in the sidebar. It's both a plugin and a widget, because it includes a drag-and-drop box that I can place anywhere the theme has added a widget area, commonly the footer and sidebar. Once I drag that widget onto my sidebar, the plugin pulls the last three (or the number I choose to display) photos I've posted.

I use and recommend WordPress for my own sites, as well as my clients'. Even if you are a large organization, it's likely the best solution for you if you want to create a professional web presence.

Your Website as a Marketing Tool

Unless your business is unusual, your website will be your primary marketing tool. It's the only piece of web "real estate" you own and control. Your social media accounts exist for the benefit of their respective companies, and could be wiped off the internet at any moment of their choosing. Your website, as long as you pay the hosting and domain name registration fees, will be live until you take it down. That's where you tell your story just as you wish with no constraints. Although each site is different based on the needs of the organizations, there are several components that no good site will go without.

About Page

If you're an individual, this page contains your biographical information and work experience. Think of your *About* page as the place where you explain to the reader why you're the best person to help them solve their problem. You want to present an excellent first impression as if this page were a virtual job interview.

For organizations, the *About* page should include your mission statement, pertinent information about your leadership and founding, what your company does and for whom. If your company history is long you may want a separate page, but don't get too enthusiastic about it; few readers are interested in a detailed history. I call my *About* page *Who I Am,* as I'm the company and it's based on my own identity.

You can divide this information up in whatever way you please as long it makes sense for the reader. For most sites, the *About* page is one of the most-read pages. Don't you want to know who you're doing business with? Give your reader everything they need to gain a sense of trust in you.

Services

This is the page I call *What I Do* on my site. It's OK to call it whatever you like as long as it clearly communicates what's there. You don't need to include prices or fees, but you should list the services you provide, and these services should be keywords.

Use benefit-focused language. If you've ever worked in sales, you understand. Years ago, I was a sales rep for a medical device manufacturer. What I remember most about my training was the differentiation between features and benefits. It's easy for most of us to get excited about the features of our products or services. We understand them and we get how fabulous they are. But your customer doesn't care about features; they care about the benefit. Always ask yourself, from the customer's point of view, "What's in it for me?" Here's an example of features vs. benefits from the Word-Press section that you read a few pages ago.

- Feature: WordPress powers 28.9 percent of the internet.
- Benefit: The fact that WordPress powers 28.9 percent of the internet gives you a strong community for support.

See the difference? Why do you care how many people use WordPress if there's nothing in it for you?

Here's another example. Say you're buying your child a bicycle:

- Feature: This bike has really cool paint colors.
- Benefit: The psychedelic paint glows when headlights hit it, so your child can easily be seen in low light — which makes it safer.

Most of us aren't going to let our kids ride their bikes after sunset, but you get the idea. That benefit is a big one, with lots of emotional impact — the safety of your child. Use the emotional benefit to engage your reader.

Think about your avatars as you prepare or edit your copy for these pages. How can you influence and draw them in emotionally? What benefits do you, your product, and your service offer that will make them more successful, more productive or help them make more money?

If they are early adopters, how can you help them stay on the cutting edge? If they love fine food and wine, how do you appeal to their sophisticated tastes? This is why it's important to spend time on your avatar and write your copy directly to them. This goes not only for web copy, but blog posts, social media updates, images, and anything you post online.

Staff Page

If you have several staff members, you may want to include a staff page with bios. Assuming, of course, that your staff members do not object to their images and information being online, but most will not. It's always more inviting to know a bit about those you'll deal with. Consider featuring staff members with interviews.

Depending on your industry, you may wish to include some personal hobbies on your bios; a favorite sports team, books, an interest in running or hiking or crossword puzzles. You'd be surprised at how seemingly trivial things can kick off or further a relationship.

I have a good friend who lives in another city. We went to high school together, though we weren't close friends. Because we knew one another in high school we connected on Facebook. Through that connection, we both realized we are fans of the same sports team and the connection grew. We're much better friends now than we ever were in high school. That's happened to me more than a few times, so think of ways you can share bits of yourself or your staff that may help others connect.

Blog

Your blog should be an integral part of your website or you risk losing the traffic it attracts. Add a link to it on your main menu or otherwise feature it prominently on your home page. I like to add at least one to three of the most recent posts on the home page, as it shows the visitor that you're always adding new content and encourages them to come back for more. We'll talk more about blogging in the next chapter.

Contact

You need a contact page to allow visitors to get in touch with you. It's not a good idea to display an email address on your website; you're issuing an open invitation for spammers to scrape your email address and put you on blast. Instead, email addresses are typically hidden behind a contact form.

Include your social media profiles, your street address if you have one, and a Google map to your location if appropriate. You may or may not need a CAPTCHA on your contact form. A *CAPTCHA* — don't we all hate them? — is an image that displays text the user must type into a form field. It prevents the form from being used by spammers. No one loves them, but they are a necessary evil.

Frequently Asked Questions (FAQ) Page

An *FAQ* page can save you time as it answers basic questions that would otherwise require a response from you or your staff. You can anticipate the questions a reader might ask and incorporate actual questions from customers and prospects.

A well-written FAQ page can help answer possible sales objections. Begin with basic questions and add to your FAQ as other inquiries come in. By the way, it's FAQ (my preference) or FAQs, never FAQ's. It's plural, not possessive. No apostrophe is needed.

Landing Pages

A *landing page* is a page specifically designed to get the reader to take a certain action. Whether it's an email signup or a purchase you're looking for, the landing page copy is designed to guide the reader toward that end. Here are a few landing page characteristics:

- **No navigation.** That's right — no menu. You want the reader 100-percent focused on your content, not looking around and deciding where to go next. The only direction you want them to move is toward your *call to action* (CTA). Your CTA answers the question, "So, what do I do with this information?" Your CTA may be *buy, sign up, learn more,* or whatever else you hope to influence your reader to do.

> A healthy amount of indexed content on your topic will show Google that you're a valuable resource.

- **Images** that capture attention and point toward the CTA. You might use a lifestyle or aspirational image, someone using the product or just a smiling, pointing person. Choose wisely and test with different images. I once ran two Facebook ads as a test; the exact same copy with different images. Results quickly told me which image did a better job of attracting clicks — it was my least favorite image. Now I regularly test different images to see which works best.

- **One CTA.** I don't mean that you can't repeat the same CTA on a page; for longer pages that's actually a good idea. But don't try to cram more than one action on a landing page. For example, if you're trying to get email signups, don't also ask them to subscribe to your blog.

There are services like Leadpages (*Leadpages.net*), that will, for a monthly fee, provide templates and an easy drag-and-drop interface to help you build landing pages. The page is hosted on their server, but, as is the case with WordPress, the page displays on your site like a standard page. It's not cheap, but if you aren't technically inclined, Leadpages or a similar service can be a lifesaver. I now build my own landing pages using a blank template that comes with my WordPress theme, but I have used Leadpages.

After the user clicks your CTA and joins your email list or otherwise completes the action you want them to take, called a *conversion,* they should be directed to a *Thank You* page. Your *Thank You* page is an opportunity to direct a now-engaged user to other ways to connect. You can include a link to subscribe to your blog, social follow links and links to anything else you might offer online.

Create a new separate landing page for any ads or promotions you may run that are directed toward a different CTA. I used to have three buttons on the home page of my site — each one for a different service I offered. They linked to unique landing pages that explained why the reader absolutely must work with me.

Other than *About, Services, FAQ, Contact,* and *Product* pages, the others are up to you. I have a page on my site for speaking, which includes talks I've given recently and a request form. You may have other special pages; WordPress allows you to create as many as you need. One site I recently finished for a client included a *Giving Back* page, which included photos and descriptions of the client's volunteer work in the community.

E-commerce

What if you want to sell items via your website? That's called *e-commerce* and you're more than likely familiar with it. Unless you're a luddite, you've probably ordered online from Amazon or any of a host of other online retailers.

WordPress functions quite well for e-commerce with the help of a plugin called WooCommerce. You can sell physical items or downloadable digital assets and the plugin will allow you to create featured products and sales. Unless you're reasonably tech savvy, you may want a professional to help you set up WooCommerce. There are many settings, and you may need style tweaks to make your product pages more consistent with the look of your site.

Before you add e-commerce to your website, consider how you'll handle payments. First you'll choose a *payment gateway* — a service that handles the credit card information and processes the payment. PayPal is perhaps the best-known payment gateway, but there are others. WooCommerce will connect to your payment gateway and take over the payment process, which saves you the costly and involved process of adding the additional security to accept payments. The software will handle shipping costs, sales tax, and allow you to feature certain products and generate coupons and special sales.

E-Commerce Setup

- Choose payment gateways.
- If you're selling physical products, decide how you will handle fulfillment and shipping.
- WooCommerce will calculate sales tax on purchases; enter the rates for your state.
- Determine the most economical shipping method and the rates for your product.
- Will you sell only in the U.S. or worldwide?

Once you've answered these questions, you're ready to set up WooCommerce. First you'll download the plugin, which is free, from *WooCommerce.com*. There may be add-ons you need that cost anywhere from $50-$100 on a yearly basis for functions such as shipping or integration with email providers such as MailChimp,

Constant Contact, and others. Once you have added the plugin, you're ready to fill in the settings for everything from sales tax and shipping to how you want your products displayed. You'll have to enter your product weight if you plan to ship physical products, and there is also an extension that allows you to sell digital downloads. WooCommerce keeps track of orders and, when integrated with your email provider, allows you to send automated messages to buyers.

Incorporate Social Media

We've talked about your website as your online home base. All of your social media bios should point to your website. When you post links to a piece of content you want your followers to know about, draw them to your website, not to another social profile. If you blog, you have a built-in way to generate links to content on your website. We'll talk more about social media in Chapter 6.

Design Considerations

Good site design is crucial. Just as you don't want to wear dated, out-of-style clothing to make an impression, the style of your website is essential to your users' perception of you and your work. It bears repeating that a website must render well on all device sizes. You cannot afford to ignore mobile phones and tablets.

WordPress users are fortunate to have a massive collection of mobile-ready templates, or themes, to choose from, so there is no excuse not to have a site that displays well on any device. Responsive sites have special code in their CSS that causes the elements to adapt their width to the changing screen size.

Color

Even though most themes provide color schemes, you're better off using your own custom colors. A good starting point for your color scheme is the colors in your logo, particularly if it is a professional design. In that case, the designer will have thought through the colors based on your business, industry, and identity. If you have a high-quality image that you plan to use as a hero image (a large image at the top of the screen that is intended to draw the reader into your site), you can pull colors from that image.

Don't choose your favorite colors, or use personal preference as a decision making tool. Your friends and family are not the best persons to ask for input; ask your customers instead. Think about how the colors will appear to your clients and prospects; your avatar(s).

Colors carry meaning, whether or not it is intended. Most banks and financial institutions use blues and greens. Green, of course, is associated with money and blue with stability and reliability. That's why most hospitals and medical centers use blue — it's perceived as stable and clean, which is crucial in the health care industry. Discount stores often use orange or yellow to communicate a bargain. Many businesses shy away from red, as no one wants to be associated with the concept of red ink, which denotes loss.

You can study color psychology in much more depth and you may find differing opinions. Observe colors and logos as you go through your day and think about what the colors say to you and what they might say to your audience.

Images

Few visitors want to read a wall of text, so break up your copy with images that highlight your business and add color and light to your pages. Some sites have hero images in the headers of each page and the images may be different on each page, consistent with what is being described on the page.

If you're concise with your copy and break up the text with images, your pages have a much higher chance of being read. Anything you can do to separate your content into easily-digestible bits will help the reader stay with you. Always prefer bullet lists over paragraphs and use subheadings liberally.

Nonprofits

Now for the opposite end of the spectrum from e-commerce: nonprofit websites. If you're a nonprofit organization, your primary objective may be to appeal to potential donors. Once you've built your avatar, you can rely on your understanding of their motivations as you prepare your website and other marketing materials. If you also use volunteers, you will need avatars for both donors and volunteers.

You'll want an online donation page, so let's examine what needs to be on your site to encourage users to donate. Your *About* page needs basic information such as your board of directors, your mission, community partners, ways to get involved (if you use volunteers) and images that show your agency in action.

More than any other sites, nonprofits need emotional, heartstring-pulling photos that move readers to support your cause. If you give them stories about people or families you have helped, and engaging images, you'll have a better chance of getting them involved. Show them the results of their support and they will be motivated to continue. Show, don't tell.

St. Jude Children's Research Hospital here in Memphis is world famous for their research and treatment of children's cancers and, with their patients' cooperation and approval, often shares heartwarming and positive stories about lives saved and enriched through their work. St. Jude raises more than $750,000,000 each year and no patient pays for their treatment or stay in Memphis. It's safe to say they are experts at telling a compelling story.

St. Jude is a notable exception to the perception of nonprofits as understaffed and underfunded. Particularly if your organization lacks a St. Jude-sized budget, social media and an effective website are non-negotiable. If you have the capacity to produce video, do it. And by capacity I mean a staffer or volunteer with a smart phone. Even if you lack the resources to have your videos professionally shot and edited, short testimonials from those who have been helped or community partners can be invaluable in engaging the public.

In all of your external communications, be especially focused on the public, on your cause, and not on your organization. Yes, you must explain what you do, and you may feature a staff page and one that describes your programs and services, but remember — you exist because of support from those who write checks. Always engage them and write to their needs and benefits.

Nonprofits often fall into the trap of posting social updates that begin with *we need* … Except in the rarest of cases, this is ineffective, as it's me-focused. No one cares what you need. Word your requests in the form of a benefit for the reader. "Spend a day making a difference" is much more powerful than "We need volunteers for a day." Offer a benefit, such as a way to make an impact, an opportunity to spend a day outdoors serving in xyz capacity, or just a chance to learn about something new. See the difference?

Measuring Results

The gold standard for measuring web traffic is a free suite of tools called Google Analytics. To set this up on your website, all you need is a Google account. If you have Gmail, you have a Google Analytics account, whether you know it or not.

To set up analytics for your website, go to *Analytics.Google.com* and log in with your Gmail account credentials. You'll be asked to enter your website, and Google will generate a couple of unique codes. One will be a tracking number, which begins with the letters UA, and the other will be a bit of code that goes in the top portion of your website. You'll also be asked to verify that you own the site.

Don't get scared by the code, all you have to do is copy and paste it. Many premium WordPress themes have a space for Google Analytics code; if not, you'll have to paste it into the head section of your website. If you're not comfortable editing these files, you can get a professional to paste it for you.

Once the code is active, it will begin tracking visits to your site and you'll begin to see trends like what time of day you have the most traffic, which pages are most popular, how long visitors stay on your site, and a host of other information.

For example, you may find that certain kinds of content draw visitors and keep them for longer than others. Or you may learn that no one clicks your CTA. Let your analytics be your guide for any changes you make on your site. This is your audience talking to you. You can and should modify your site based on feedback by your visitors.

Google Analytics is a powerful tool and can be complex and intimidating. Google provides training and tutorials on the basics to advanced features, so you can learn all you need to know on your own — and it's all free.

Monitoring and Maintenance

It's not over when the design is finalized and the pages are up and running on the web. Just like your car, your website must be maintained. Maintenance is not generally a large time investment, but if neglected the resulting problem can be.

For WordPress users, plugins must be kept up to date. Remember that plugins are software, and software is vulnerable to *malware,* scripts or programs that are created to do harm. Updates to plugins are often security-related *patches,* or fixes, to stay ahead of new hacks, and sometimes new versions to stay compatible with the latest Word-Press update. Reputable developers update their plugins frequently.

> More than 50 percent of Word-Press website hacks are due to outdated plugins.

One important factor when choosing a plugin is how long ago it's been since the developer updated it; the more recent, the better. You can see the date of the creator's last update on the plugin download page. According to WP Template, more than 50 percent of WordPress hacks are due to outdated plugins.[6]

In addition to plugin updates, it's important to keep up with WordPress updates. These are also often security updates, but may add extra functionality, improve on existing features, or fix bugs. Although it's relatively rare, a WordPress update can break themes or plugins if they are not compatible with the new version.

Themes must be updated and the same security concerns apply to themes as to plugins. Unless you've made changes to the theme files themselves, theme updates shouldn't affect your site. Rather than updating actual theme files, it's best to create a *child theme,* which is a copy of edited files placed in a separate folder inside the themes folder on the server with the parent theme. You won't need to know this if you're not editing theme files, but it's good to understand the concept.

Updating a theme is as simple as clicking a link, but before you update it's important to perform a full backup of your site, just in case something goes wrong. If the worst happens, you'll be able to revert easily to the previous version. It's a great idea to have daily backups, especially if you change your site frequently.

In addition to theme, plugin, and WordPress updates, keep your content up to date. Be sure you incorporate any changes in your business or offerings into the site. Your website won't be helpful to anyone if it's out of date and it won't represent you well.

Consider your website one of your most important assets and treat it accordingly. I once had a prospective client ask to meet with me about a website. The meeting was over quickly when he told me his budget for the entire site was $500. Yes, you can get a $500 website, but you'll get what you pay for. Don't be cheap; hire a professional who knows what they are doing. You need good design, understanding of online marketing, attention to detail, and a site that is customized for your organization. Your business reputation is worth putting your best foot forward.

Plan to update and/or redesign your site every three to four years, depending on your industry. Sites that looked great three years ago now look dated and out of style. Just like you wouldn't go to a job interview in a baby blue leisure suit from the 70s, don't allow your website to become a liability. Keep it current and running smoothly and safely and remember — it's often a potential customer's first impression. Keep your first impression sleek and professional.

4

Blogging

Why Should I Blog?

Blogging Stats[7]

- 55 percent more website visitors with a blog
- 97 percent more incoming links
- 434 percent more pages indexed by Google

There are several ways users find your website. They may follow a link from another site, such as a social media profile, go directly to your site from an offline marketing piece, via word of mouth, or through a search engine. Research shows that search engines may be responsible for more than 60 percent of your total traffic.[8]

Because search engines are such a large source of traffic, it's important to consider the factors that help your site rank highly in search results. Most websites can benefit from the addition of a blog and here are three compelling reasons you should include a blog on your website:

1. **Traffic Increase** — The more content on your site related to your desired keywords, the more Google's bots will discover and index on your site. A healthy amount of indexed content on your topic will show Google that you're a valuable resource. Research shows that for business-to-business (B2B) marketers, those who have blogs get 67 percent more leads.[9] An excellent blog is a great way to draw traffic to your website and regularly updated, quality content will reward you with higher rankings in search results. As a side note, when I mention Google search, I don't literally mean only Google, I'm referring to all search engines. It's just that Google's market share of search traffic is far more than any other. This doesn't mean you should neglect other search engines, but as this isn't an SEO course and I'm no SEO expert, I'll leave it to them to cover the others.

2. **Build Thought Leadership** — An excellent blog is not only a great way to draw traffic to your website, it helps you establish yourself as an expert and a resource for valuable information to make your customers' lives easier. Blogging helps build authority. The more information you publish about your subject matter, the more you're seen as an expert. As we discussed in the

Introduction, building thought leadership is the process of making yourself the go-to person on a particular topic. I want to emphasize that quality is superior to quantity. Every time you publish a post that solves a reader's problem, you build authority and thought leadership. Google repeatedly emphasizes that the best way to rank higher is a high volume of quality content, rather than trying to game the system.

3. **Build Customer/Client Relationships** — Blogs have a much more personal touch than websites. They can give you information about the product or ways to use the product without being salesy. Your readers and prospects see a different side of your business; the more human side. You can give your audience a behind-the-scenes look at how the sausage is made, so to speak.

Here's a great example. Pat Flynn, a noted author, speaker, and blogger, produces the popular *Smart Passive Income*[10] podcast and website. He's done quite well for himself and consistently publishes helpful content that teaches others to do what he's done — make money online by creating products that meet customers' needs.

Pat did an in-depth post on how to get started with podcasting a few years ago. It includes several videos and gets very detailed, even down to specific microphones and other equipment you'll need. It's a must-read if you're interested in podcasting, and, in the course of my online reading, I've found that many other experts cite Pat's post as a source. If you do a Google search on how to start podcasting, you'll probably find Pat's link at number two, just behind a paid ad. Pat has built strong thought leadership and an excellent Google rank on the topic of podcasting via this post.

While the initial post was written in 2012, the principles still apply, so if you're into podcasting, read Pat's post. Even if you're not interested in podcasting it's a great example of thought leadership.

While you're informing and educating, you're also showing your relatable side. Don't we all want to do business with people we know and like? This is not a new idea; we've always chosen those we like to give our business to. Large chains often provide lower prices, but still many of us choose smaller establishments because of the relationships we have built.

If you've ever watched old sitcoms like Andy Griffith, this is a familiar sentiment. No self-respecting Mayberry gentleman would think of going anywhere besides Floyd's Barber Shop for their shave and haircut. Blogging allows you to let your customers in and build that Floyd-the-Barber loyalty.

If you still need convincing, Impact, an inbound marketing agency has a great post that summarizes why a blog is crucial to building traffic, which you can find at *Impactbnd.com*; search for *55 Reasons Blogging Creates More Traffic*.[11]

How Do I Start a Blog?

Brainstorm Content

Before you begin to think about platforms or any of the technical aspects of blogging, spend some time brainstorming content. Get out that list of keywords — remember the words you want to be found for online? Don't write a word of a post or do one bit of design or layout work on a blog before you've spent considerable time refining your content ideas.

I say this from experience. In 2006 I started blogging. At the time, blogging was still relatively new and I was a stay-at-home mom whose oldest daughter was leaving for college in a few months. I often say I started blogging because it was cheaper than a psychiatrist. My purpose for writing was pure self expression. You'll never read those first few posts; thankfully they've long since been taken down and no one will ever be bored by them again.

Through the years, I began to write more about things I cared about, and when I began to do freelance work the website became as much of an online portfolio as a blog. It has changed many times through the years, as I try to keep it current and timely.

About three or four years ago, I looked at my blog/website with fresh eyes. I was horrified. It was a mess of too many categories, not enough tags, and no organization. One post might be about my kid leaving for college, the next a social media how-to post. No one knew what to expect. Don't be like me. Have the purpose of your blog clear in your mind before you ever put fingers to keyboard, so that your reader knows why they are there.

Let's talk about the structure of a blog. I mentioned the CMS in the last chapter. A CMS allows you to publish your own content and sort it into categories. For example, on my website, my categories are *social media, WordPress, writing,* and *small business.* These are the four buckets my content naturally falls into — the areas in which I focus my work. Think about your own buckets, or categories.

Choose three to five categories. They should either be keywords or be closely related to your keywords and topics on which you can easily create content. Think through potential posts that will fit into these categories and attract the audience you have targeted.

One of my favorite examples of how to do blogging well is Whole Foods. Their blog is consistently full of helpful recipes and ideas for customers (or prospects) to make life easier. During the holiday season their blog featured decorating and gift ideas, as well as a post about a certain type of fish and tips on how to prepare it. Whole Foods is an excellent brand to follow online all the way around; they do a fantastic job of engaging their audience on social media sites, and their website is the one of the most reader focused I've ever seen.

Whole Foods' blog is cited in numerous "best blogs" lists. Here's why: they have mastered the art of reader-focused content. They regularly post articles about food, home decor, recipes, and many other forms of content that don't seek to sell products, but to establish themselves as a source of helpful information. They do include a call to action in most posts, but it's not hard sell, and by the time you see it, you've already enjoyed the content.

What Do I Write About?

Now that you've seen the benefit of adding a blog to your site, where do you start? Go back to your keywords. Remember, these words and phrases reflect what you want to be found for online, so the content you produce should naturally fall into place.

The best blog content, like Whole Foods', is reader focused. That means you're not writing about yourself or your business, but you're thinking about what your avatar(s) want and need to read. Here are some ideas for stimulating your creative mind:

Customer questions are gold in the palm of your hand as they take you directly to your customers' pain points. Surveys can help you pinpoint topics your readers want to know more about. Add a feedback button to your website and respond to any suggestions you receive (at least the reasonable ones). It shows your visitors you care about what they think and need.

Incorporate conversations and questions from discussions on social media sites or ask your followers to suggest the kind of content they wish to read.

Types of Content

Blog content can come in different forms. Don't get stuck thinking you always have to write 2000 words. Here are some ideas about what can constitute a blog post:

- **Lists.** List posts, sometimes called *listicles,* are and have been popular for some time. Post titles with numbers typically draw more interest, so try *10 Ways to Bathe a Cat* in list form rather than regular prose.
- **A video.** Do a short tutorial on a tip or technique. You can do this easily with screencasting software such as ScreenFlow (Mac) or Camtasia (PC). I've used Screen-Flow for numerous how-to videos and its learning curve is quite reasonable.
- **An interview.** You can do this as a written interview, or use audio or video. Or both, as some visitors may prefer to read a written transcript while others would rather watch a video.
- **Images.** Infographics are a great way to add content from others. Readers like seeing information presented visual-

ly; if you're a talented designer you can make your own. *Canva.com* is a great resource for many types of images and you can use it completely free. You can also embed graphics from other sources if you don't have design talents. If you do, add a few words of your own to explain what you think makes the infographic valuable.

- **Profiles.** Do a customer profile. MileIQ is a mobile app that helps professionals keep track of business mileage. After I did a blog post about the service, tweeted it, and tagged the company, they asked if I'd be willing to do a quick interview for a customer profile. It's an excellent way to recognize valuable customers and give them a reason to be loyal.

- **Polls.** Ask a question and review the answers. Now that Twitter and Facebook provide poll functionality, it's simple to do. If you're a WordPress user, it's easy to incorporate polls on your website, chart the results, and write a post what you learned.

- **Sureys.** Much like polls, surveys give you a peek into the reader's mind. Online tools like Survey Monkey and Google Forms allow you to create surveys that you can post to your website, send to your email list, and publish on social media sites. Surveys are usually more in-depth than polls, and include more than one question.

- **Special occasions.** Take advantage of holidays big and small. You can find lists online of all kinds of holidays, from New Year's Day to National Chocolate-Covered Anything Day. Particularly if it relates to your content, it can be a fun post.

- **Behind the scenes.**
  Everyone loves a be-
  hind-the-scenes look.
  For example, if you're
  a photographer, have
  someone take pictures

> If you solve customers' prob-
> lems in a way that is authen-
> tic and shows you care about
> them ... they will fall in love
> with you.

  of a shooting session and post. Or post photos of your
  studio and props.

- **Show your human side.** Sometimes a more personal
  photo can give your readers a glimpse of who you are as
  a human being; and we all prefer to do business with human beings. Depending on your niche, if you can incorporate appropriate pieces of your personal life into your
  posts, your readers will see you as a real person.

- **Special days of the week.** Maybe you set aside Friday to
  post fun stuff — for example, Fifi Friday would be a great
  way to feature the office canine. Show her in a company
  t-shirt or seasonal outfit. #MotivationMonday is a popular Twitter hashtag, where users post inspiring, uplift-
  ing content — such as tips for getting healthy, business
  success, etc.

Here's a mental exercise that might help as we think about blog
content. Let's say you own a fruit stand, and you want to start a blog
to reach more customers. What keywords would you choose?

Fruit, Buy fruit, Lemons, Oranges, Apples, Bananas, Mangos

Bear in mind that in the real world, you would have to pay
Google a king's ransom in advertising fees; these keywords would

be extremely difficult to rank for organically. They are far too common (read: expensive) for our fruit stand to rank organically. With those caveats in mind, let's go on with our example. Add some long-tail keywords such as best fresh fruit in <insert city>.

Fresh fruit in New York is more specific than *fruit*.

Fresh lemons in New York would be even more specific.

You'll get less traffic with long-tail keywords, but the traffic you do get will be better qualified — that is, they'll be searching for exactly what you're selling. This boosts your chances of making a conversion — remember, that's a sale or other desired action by the user in the online marketing world.

Consider the categories of content you'll use on your blog. Depending on your topic and subject matter, your categories may be more general or specific. It's great if you can use keywords as your category names.

Your CMS will sort your posts into the categories you designate and you'll use tags to sort even more specifically. Let's think about how to set up our categories for our fruit blog. You might have categories like *Recipes That Use Fruit, Special Seasonal Fruits,* and *Cooking Techniques for Fruit.*

You see that these categories are reader focused. They are created to help the reader enjoy fruit — giving in some way. This is blogging done well and it will be much more effective than trying to sell overtly.

How Not to Blog

Many years ago I had a client who thought a blog would help his business. I agreed and we discussed ideas for posts. He was enthusiastic about blogging and I was excited when I received his first post.

It didn't take long for that excitement to wear off. What he had written could have been copy for a promotional brochure. It was an entire post on why we are the best, what we do better than our competition … all about us.

He missed the point. Anything you post that could be placed on a brochure or ad for your business is an indication you're doing it wrong. A blog is not for selling or telling. Your singular focus must be the reader. Try to explain why your customers should choose you over the competition or why you're unique and you'll alienate the ones you want to reach. People know when they're being sold to and they hate it. Don't you?

When you're planning content, don't ask, "What do I want to tell them about me?" — ask "What problem does my customer or prospective customer have that I can help them solve?" That's being reader focused and it's the only way you'll find success in blogging. If you solve your customers' problems in a way that is authentic and shows you truly care about them, you won't have to write brochure copy because they will fall in love with you.

The Technical Stuff

Choose Your Platform

I've already discussed my preference for WordPress, but there are other popular platforms for blogging, among them Tumblr, Wix, and Squarespace. I urge you to investigate all other options and determine what's best for you. You have two choices when it comes to blogging.

- Free hosted blogs like Tumblr and *WordPress.com*.
- Self hosted: WordPress (there are others but that's for another book).

Free Hosted — The free hosted blogs cost nothing to set up unless you want to use your own domain name, for example *Your-Name.com* instead of *YourName.Tumblr.com*. You pay to register the domain name itself, which varies in price. Some platforms are limited, but may be right for you if you're just starting out and have limited resources. If you don't feel comfortable dealing with web hosting, or don't have someone with these skills available this can be the way to go. Hosted blogs are perfect for those who aren't using it for business and want a simple personal blog. With a free hosted blog, you open an account, name your blog, decide on a theme (template) and color scheme, start writing and you're good to go.

The advantages of this solution are that it takes little time or resources and allows you to get your blog up and running quickly. The downside is that you often have little control over design, and limited flexibility on the functionality you can add. For this reason, I do not recommend a free hosted solution for a business website.

Self Hosted — I believe WordPress self hosted is the go-to solution for a business website. With the self-hosted version you provide your own server through a web hosting service such as Bluehost, Dreamhost, Siteground, Godaddy, WP Engine, or many others. Web hosting can cost between $6/month for economy hosting and $30/month for managed WordPress hosting that includes daily backups. For larger sites and those with heavy traffic you may spend more. Your budget will determine what sort of hosting you choose, and if you're just starting and don't have a huge amount of traffic, economy hosting can work just fine. While it's OK to get started with less expensive hosting, plan to upgrade as soon as you can afford the extra money, as your site's performance will probably improve markedly with better hosting.

The reason WordPress is free and will always be free is that it is *open source software*. Open source means that the source code is freely available for anyone to modify and redistribute.

Once you secure your hosting, you'll install WordPress on your server. Just like Microsoft Office runs on your computer and gives you word processing and spreadsheet capabilities, WordPress is installed on your server and allows you to run your website. Before you purchase a hosting package, ensure that your host is WordPress compatible. If so, they should have a one-click install option. This is easy peasy, as the installer will automatically create the necessary components for you and connect it to WordPress. Once WordPress is installed, you'll be able to set up your site and you'll have unlimited control over the look, feel, and functionality of your site.

When I teach groups about the difference between *WordPress. com* and *WordPress.org,* I find it helpful to use the house analogy I used in the website chapter. Let's say you move to a new town and rent a house. You like it well enough but would like to make some changes. Depending on your agreement with the landlord, you may be able to paint walls, and you can certainly add rugs, drapes, and hang pictures as you like. What if you wish the kitchen were bigger? You can't knock down walls or make structural changes. So, although it's your home and it may function perfectly well, you don't have complete freedom to customize it to your preferences.

Your website is the same. A self-hosted site gives you ownership of every facet of your website. You can knock down walls and make any structural changes you like. Even if you start with a hosted site, self hosted should be the goal you work toward as your website grows and becomes more of a marketing asset.

Design

Most platforms allow you some control over the look of your site. Even the free services allow you to choose different templates, or *themes.* You can change the color scheme, fonts, and make basic layout modifications.

If you're self hosting, the sky's the limit. You can install a theme and use it out of the box, hire a designer to create a custom theme, or go somewhere in between with an existing theme that's custom-ized for your brand. Obviously the more custom your solution, the more it's going to cost, so keep budget in mind. Most small businesses can do quite well with a customized existing theme and appropriate add-ons for any additional functionality you need.

Your Blog and Your Website

I've seen businesses create a separate site for their blog, which draws the reader away from the website. The best solution is to in-corporate the blog into the website, which extends the SEO benefits of blogging to your entire site. Most websites are hybrids of a blog and a website and that's easy to do with WordPress, which allows you to add nearly anything to your site navigation.

Step 5

Content Marketing

Unless you live under a rock with no wifi, you've probably heard the term *content marketing,* which simply means you attract customers with content. It can take many forms, one of which is your blog. It can also be whitepapers, guides, ebooks, or even print publications.

The content is not sales copy — far from it. Once I stumbled onto a YouTube video that taught me how to reupholster a chair. The only sales copy the company included in the video was the occasional popup that provided a link to purchase the tools the upholsterer was using. I found the links helpful, as I was well into the content when they began to appear. It wasn't their promotional talk that made me want to buy — it was the skill of the team member, the potential cost savings and the prospect of better-looking living room that inspired me. Though I'm not ready to start the project now, I subscribed to their email newsletter, which keeps them top of mind. I'll certainly go back to them when I am prepared to start the project. That's good content marketing.

Hubspot, a provider of marketing software for businesses, has long been a winner at content marketing. Not only do they consistently post valuable content, their Hubspot Academy allows you to learn more about marketing topics in the form of online courses, all free. They've done a tremendous job of establishing themselves as a resource for marketing needs and questions, and the sheer volume of content makes it likely that they'll turn up in a search for nearly any online-marketing-related term.

Content marketing sounds great, but it's a tall order, right? How do I make this happen for my business? Like any other business idea, you scale it to your resources. If you're a staff of one, you won't produce a 2000-word blog post each day in addition to everything else on your plate. Be realistic as you consider what you can do.

It's OK to start modestly. Be consistent in posting, as this helps keep your traffic coming and your readers begin to expect to hear from you. If you can manage one post every two weeks, that's a great place to start. You can increase your frequency as you get more comfortable with the process. Keep it coming — it doesn't have to be a precise schedule, but some regularity is a good thing.

If you have staff who are good writers or have social media skills, assign them to generate ideas, write posts, and share on social media. Keep a close eye on what they are publishing and approve their posts before they are published. If it's going out over your name, it's ultimately your tail on the line, not theirs.

If your team lacks the skills, you may need to hire a freelance blogger or social media consultant. If you go this route, it's important that they understand your industry, your company culture, and are able to speak the language. Be prepared to pay for their expertise and time to research topics in your field. There's a reason you don't have time to do it yourself.

I once had a client whose field I didn't understand. As much as I love to write and learn new things, I thought I'd be able to research and learn on the go, but it was far more complicated than I had anticipated. I resigned that gig because I knew I could not do it justice. On the other hand, there's another organization, a nonprofit that I've been involved with long enough that I know the culture like an insider. I can write far more successfully for them than for my former client. No one can write about your business like you can, but that's not always feasible. If you have to outsource your content creation, take the time to find a writer who gets you, understands your audience and can speak intelligently about your business.

Editorial Calendar

One area in which I've only too recently begun to take my own advice is the creation of an editorial calendar. Your content will be most effective when it's planned in advance and you won't be caught unaware when a holiday or special day comes up.

Here in Memphis our area code is 901, so September 1 is known as *901 Day* — when we celebrate what's good about our city. For 901 Day one year, I did a list post — *10 Things I Love About the 901*. It performed quite well, and I resolved to do something similar this year. Unfortunately I missed it — not because I didn't know that September 1 follows August 31, but because I didn't plan. If I had added the date to my editorial calendar, I'd have seen that in advance and written a post.

You can use something as simple as a Google spreadsheet, or CoSchedule, which may be emerging as the industry standard for editorial calendar planning, though it's a paid solution. It's used and recommended by many experts, but pricing plans start at $39/ month. For your money, CoSchedule not only helps you plan your blog posts, but guides you as you build a social media campaign. There's a free WordPress integration that connects CoSchedule to your website. (I have no affiliation with CoSchedule beyond having done their trial membership.)

Google Calendar is free and can be an effective tool — I might have started with it if I'd thought about it, if only for the ability to set reminders. Whatever your solution, you'll want to incorporate your blog posts into your posting schedule for those platforms.

When I started my editorial calendar, I had no idea where to begin. There were several false starts until I finally came up with the Google spreadsheet I now use. It isn't perfect but at least it gives me a starting point for planning. You may prefer good old-fashioned pen and paper and that's OK. An online presence that is planned and coordinated will be much more effective than a scattershot approach. I added the list of special holidays to my calendar, just in case one might fit into a post and draw extra traffic from its hashtag.

You may be thinking about the time it takes to write and pub- lish original content and wondering how you're going to find the time to produce enough to fill a social media profile. Few people or organizations can generate enough original content. So we turn to others' content that fits our message and purpose.

Most marketers combine their original posts with curation of others' content. Like a museum curator, you're finding and gathering information that will interest your audience and presenting it to them in a way that's easy to digest.

Reading other blogs is an excellent way to get inspiration for your own and stay up on popular topics. You can find and share content that benefits your readers and helps you highlight others while you're growing your own online presence. Share often enough and, you never know, they may return the favor.

How To Find Great Content

My favorite tool for content discovery is *Feedly.com*. Feedly aggregates posts from blogs so that you don't have to go looking for their content. You can do a search for your topic and subscribe to blogs that fit. Feedly brings them right to you so you don't have to search. Though they offer a paid plan, you can use Feedly without paying. Use keyword alerts to have Feedly find content that fits a keyword you enter, or use the hints and tags they provide to find content. All you have to do is click *Follow* to add the feed to your account.

After you add the feed, new posts will show up in your dashboard. You can create folders to organize your topics. Depending on how the source feed is configured, you may see the entire post in Feedly or you may have to click through to read it. Either way, you can save it for later if you like. In addition to saving, there are share buttons that allow you to send the post to LinkedIn, Twitter, WordPress, save it to Evernote or send it to a scheduler such as Buffer (we'll talk more about Buffer later).

When you're ready to read your content, go to *Feedly.com* and log in. Upon login, you'll be taken to the Dashboard where you'll see the content from your chosen sources.

Other sources of content are Alltop (*Alltop.com*), BuzzSumo (*BuzzSumo.com*), and Flipboard (*Flipboard.com*). Both Feedly and Flipboard have particularly lovely mobile apps, which means even when you're waiting somewhere you can be finding content to save and share. For more on content curation, I have a video that details my process on my Vimeo profile, called *How I Curate Content*.

Once you get into the groove, your social presence will feature a combination of original and curated content. Of course, the more original posts you can manage the better, but boosting others is a great way to build relationships and get noticed online.

Writing and Grammar

Let's talk a little about grammar, punctuation, and spelling. Nothing undermines authority like poor sentence structure or a misplaced apostrophe. The other day I was about to share a great article when I noticed a misplaced apostrophe. No go.

When you're writing for the web or any marketing material, use the inverted pyramid method; put the most important points near the top in case your reader doesn't make it to the end. Write tightly and eliminate unnecessary words like *that, very, really,* and *actually.* You may have seen the abbreviation *TL;DR* — it means *too long, didn't read.* If you've written a very long post, you might summarize the takeaways at the top with a TL;DR and the main idea.

Get familiar with the *AP Stylebook*, which will give you guid-ance on hyphenation, capitalization, how to style government agencies, titles, institutions, and virtually anything else you need to express in writing. You don't have to follow AP to the letter; it's OK to make your own exceptions as long as you're consistent.

> Nothing undermines authority like poor sentence structure or a misplaced apostrophe.

I recommend the online subscription, which is searchable. If you work as part of a team, put your styles in writing where they differ from AP and be sure the team has access to a stylebook. For example, I follow AP almost 100 percent, however, unlike AP, I do use and recommend the Oxford (or serial) comma for clarity. Using a style guide helps keep your writing consistent and professional.

The First Content Marketer

I want to end this chapter with one of my favorite content marketing stories. Perhaps the first content marketer was a man named John Deere. Yeah, the tractor guy. This story was related by Joe Pulizzi in his book, *Epic Content Marketing: How to Tell a Different Story, Break Through the Clutter, and Win More Customers By Marketing Less,* McGraw-Hill Education. Kindle Edition in Chapter 2.[12]

In 1836, John, a blacksmith from New England, was young and broke. He needed to provide for his family, so he made the desperate decision to leave his family to go west to find work. He had $73 in his pocket when he set out, and two weeks later he ended up in Grand Detour, Illinois. He started a blacksmith business, and every day he heard the same stories of farmers who had come from the Northeast struggling to push their plows through the sticky Illinois soil.

The iron plows used in New England couldn't push through the Midwest's sod and the farmers had to stop and clean the mud off the plows every few yards. John had an idea. What if he could mold the outside of the plow in steel? The mud and dirt wouldn't stick to the steel. So he built the first polished plow using a broken saw blade.

The response was positive and John continued to build his business. He worked closely with the farmers, listened to their feedback and modified his product accordingly. Over time, his product changed to become more aligned with his customers' needs and, as a result, his business grew. Deere knew if he could make the farmers' work easier, they would be loyal buyers.

John Deere passed away in 1886, but his values of listening and teaching live on through the company he built. Deere & Company, arguably the most famous agricultural company in the world, launched, created, and distributed *The Furrow* magazine in 1895. Deere leveraged *The Furrow,* not to sell John Deere equipment directly as a catalog would, but to educate farmers on new technology and how they could be more successful.

From the beginning, *The Furrow* was not filled with promotional messages and self-serving content. It was developed by thoughtful journalists, storytellers, and designers, and covered topics that farmers cared about. The goal of the content was to help farmers become more prosperous and, of course, profitable.

The Furrow is still going strong, 120 years later. It is the largest circulated farming magazine in the world. John Deere is often given credit for being the first to leverage content marketing as part of a long-term business process.

John Deere, the first content marketer.

6

Social Media

Today's customers and clients want to interact with you before they spend their money. Although the term *Web 2.0,* which described a new, more interactive internet is outdated and has fallen into disuse, online interaction has only grown. With today's websites and the prevalence of social media, we now have the ability to communicate directly with our customers.

Social media is not without risk. Any time you make yourself visible on the internet you run the risk of negative feedback. Don't fear it. Embrace it and let it make you better. Businesses, both online and brick and mortar, can get valuable customer feedback through social media. While negative comments may do nothing for your ego, the insights can be worth the indignity. Once you know you have a problem, you have the opportunity to fix it and show that you care about your customer's experience, and that you'll listen even if it's painful. When you do, you'll earn back your customers' trust and loyalty.

Let's say you own a restaurant and someone comes in on a bad night and gives you a terrible review on Facebook. You can delete it and try to forget or you can respond, learn from it, and show your customer you're interested in their experience and want to make it better.

Apologize, acknowledge the issue, and give them a gift certificate for a free meal and they will love you. In addition, the rest of your Facebook fans will watch this play out and they will know that you listen to your customers.

Social networking is about conversation, engagement, and relationship building. It is not advertising or selling. Don't blast your followers about your fabulous product. Building a following is not instantaneous; you will not set up a Twitter account one day and make a million dollars the next. It is not about you when you're doing it right — it's about helping others and contributing to their lives.

I've often referred to social media as an online cocktail party. I hope you wouldn't go to a cocktail party with a fistful of business cards, foist them on some poor unsuspecting person and back them into a corner with your sales pitch.

You won't make a lasting connection at a cocktail party, but you may connect with someone you'd like to get to know better. If you do it right you'll make a great first impression and learn more about the other person than they do about you. It's the very same on social networks. If you're too salesy, you'll get unfollowed; if you're friendly and helpful you'll do well.

Pew Research, an organization that conducts polls, research, and analysis about "trends shaping America and the world," re-leased the results of a study of online adults who use social media, which shows the popularity of various social platforms.[13]

- Facebook   79%
- LinkedIn   29%
- Twitter   24%
- Pinterest   31%
- Instagram   32%
- Snapchat   31%[14]

When Pew first began tracking social media use by adults in 2005, only five percent of Americans used a social media platform; by 2011 the percentage had grown to half. As of January 2017, 69 percent of all Americans use at least one social media platform.[15]

It may not surprise you that Facebook wins by a landslide. The next most popular platforms are Snapchat, Pinterest, Instagram, LinkedIn, and Twitter. I show these figures because I think it's instructive to examine where the other social networks fall on the spectrum. Consider that, depending on your industry and the de-mographics of your audience, you might get a completely different result if you did a similar survey.

The next section will explore eight social networks in depth and discuss how to make the best use of each.

Facebook

Let's get started with Facebook, which we know is by far the most popular. To put things in perspective, Facebook has more active users than China's entire population (which is estimated to be 1.40 billion).[16] If you're active on Facebook, you have a personal profile. This is how you connect with friends and family and post those photos of your dog, your vacation, and the food you're about to eat.

In 2007, Facebook introduced business pages, which provided a more suitable presentation for businesses than a personal profile. Instead of friends, those who were interested in your business became fans, which Facebook changed to *likes* a few years ago. Through the years, Facebook has added contests, ads, and storefronts that allow businesses to sell on the platform.

Facebook has more active users than China's entire population (which is estimated to be 1.40 billion).

In the beginning, it was relatively easy to reach your audience, draw likes, and have your content seen by those who liked your page. That's now simply not the case. It's extremely difficult to gain organic reach; remember Facebook is a company whose goal is to make a profit. They do that very effectively through advertising sales. Other than paid advertising, the best you can do is to post content that gets responses and engagement from those who see it — this is the only way you'll have any hope of organic reach — and it still will probably not be enough.

Users who complain about Facebook's frequent layout and feature changes would do well to remember that Facebook's users aren't their customers — we are the product. Advertisers, who are buying our eyes on their ads, are their customers. The changes reflect Facebook's desire to keep users engaged so that we will stay longer and view more ads.

Still, Facebook is where the majority of your customers probably are, so in most cases you should maintain a presence. You may eventually have to budget at least a small amount for advertising, but take heart, Facebook advertising is much less expensive than Google ads.

Page Setup

If you want to build a Facebook business page, you'll also have to keep a personal profile, as you create and maintain your page via the administrative role assigned through your page. When you create the page, you'll automatically be an administrator; you can add others as you wish. There are different roles you can assign based on the amount of freedom you wish to give each administrator to post.

Once you log in to Facebook via your personal profile, you'll see links to create ads, pages, and groups at the bottom of the left column. The link takes you to a screen where you'll select the type of page you want to create. Your choices are:

- **Local Business or Place:** This is ideal for brick and mortar businesses, where you want customers to come to your physical location. You'll be asked to provide an address. There is a list of business categories to choose from, and you'll also be prompted to enter hours and parking information. Visitors will be able to check in, which lets their friends know they are at your location.

- **Company Organization or Institution:** Perhaps you have more than one location, with varying hours, or you're an e-commerce business and only sell products on your own website. This type of page will work well for you; you have the option to allow customers to check in at your location.

- **Brand or Product:** This page type is for you if you're a brand that sells products through many retailers. Examples are Nike, Oreo, Coca-Cola, and numerous other large brands you recognize.
- **Artist, Band, or Public Figure:** This page is focused on promoting you and your work. Well-known politicians, musical groups, artists, or actors use this page type.
- **Entertainment:** An entertainment page works best for you if your business is a form of entertainment; book pages, movie pages, television show pages fall under this category.
- **Cause or Community:** This is the only page type that has no categories. If you're a local nonprofit or other organization with a physical location, you're better off using a local business page.

It's worth going through each page type and its categories to decide which one works best for you. You can always change your page type or category.

Now that you've got the page established, it's time for the fun part — the photos. The first thing you need is a profile photo, which appears at the top left of your page. This should be a photo that is instantly recognizable and associated with your identity. You can use your logo if you like, as long as it's an image people will associate with you. Make it easy to see; don't use group photos or photos taken from a distance. Since I am my business, I use a headshot for my business profile photo. If you use a headshot, make sure your face is recognizable and visible.

To the right of the profile photo is the cover photo. Its size is 851 by 315 pixels. Be creative with your cover photo. As of this writing, mine is a promotional image for this book. You can make the cover photo link to any page you like by using the description. In the past, I've added a fake button to the image; just add a circle or other button-like shape in an image editing program like Photoshop and add a CTA. This reminds the reader that the cover photo is clickable.

Where you place the fake button on the image makes no difference; the entire photo links to the photo page with its description. Don't waste this opportunity to add a line or two about your business, then a link to your website. My cover photo links to a special landing page that is a sales page for this book.

There is a built-in CTA button under the cover photo. You can choose from numerous calls to action; I use *Learn More* as my goal is to drive traffic to the landing page.

Fill out your *About* section, linked in the left column under the *Home* link, especially including your website and other social networks. Include the description of your business (using keywords), contact information, and location if you're using a page that facilitates it. Select a recognizable username for your page, so that you can easily tell people where to find you.

Under the *About* link, you see more subpages. You can arrange them in whatever order you like. If you use a lot of video, make it more prominent, but you generally want the *About* section as high as possible on the page.

Once you have finished your page setup, start adding content. I like to add a few posts so that the page looks less empty before I tell everyone about the page. You can backdate content to help you fill the page more quickly.

Add posts to your Facebook page in the same way as you add them to your profile. To add a link, paste in the *URL,* which stands for *uniform resource locator,* and is simply the web address. It should autofill with a thumbnail photo and the title of the post you're linking to. If it doesn't autofill, add a related photo via the upload link. Once the preview image shows up, you can delete the text link for a cleaner look. It's a good idea to make a comment that indicates why you think the post is valuable.

When you have added a few posts, start inviting your friends to like your page. Just under your cover photo you'll see a button with three dots. Click that button and you'll see a dropdown with links to page settings, the ability to view your page as a visitor, and a link to invite friends to like your page. Click on the *Invite* link and add the friends you think may be interested. Most people who know you will not mind being asked and will like your page.

An hour or so after you've posted, just under your posts, you'll see the word *Reach* and a number. Your reach for a particular post is the number of users the post has been shown to. Don't feel like a failure if your reach is far below the number of users who like your page. It takes time to build up reach; it's based on engagement, such as likes, comments, and shares. More engagement means Facebook will show your post to more users. No one but you or another page admin can see the reach numbers, or tell which personal profile your posts come from.

You can choose to receive notifications when someone likes

or comments on a post on your page. I like to receive those notifi-cations on Facebook so I don't miss the opportunity to engage. If you're on Facebook frequently choose Facebook notifications rather than email; it will be far less annoying.

What to Post

If you have a business blog, of course you'll want to add each new post to your Facebook page, but you don't have to wait for a new post. You can post content from others that benefits your audi-ence; such as photos and videos from any events you may hold or sponsor. Solicit your readers to post their own photos while using, wearing, or otherwise associating with your product. Ask questions. Create polls. Look for motivational quotes — some of my posts with the best reach have been quotes laid over background images.

To maximize your reach on Facebook you'll have to pay, howev-er, there are things you can do to boost your organic reach.

Three Tips to Help You Maximize Organic Reach

- Post when your audience is active online — you'll find this information in your *Insights*.
- Test different types of content to see which resonates best with your audience. They may prefer video or a simple link post, but you don't know until you test. Video blows everything else away with my audience, so when I have time I make a short one.
- Always include an image. Photos get 53 percent more likes, 104 percent more comments and 84 percent more click-throughs on links than text-based posts.[17]

Scheduling Posts

Facebook allows you the option of scheduling your posts for a later date. As you enter the copy for your post, a blue *Publish* button will appear with a dropdown to the right. That dropdown contains options to schedule your post for a later time, backdate it, or save it in draft. Use the backdate option if you're trying to populate a new page with content before you invite others to like your page. You can also use third-party services such as Hootsuite or Buffer to schedule posts to your page. Although there have been reports that posts from third-party services are penalized, a 2016 article from Buffer (consider the source)[18] asserts that there is no penalty. I've repeatedly tested posting from Buffer vs. from Facebook and I can't see a difference, but now I post directly from Facebook just in case.

Posting frequency depends on your audience and industry, but most pages shouldn't post more than twice each day. Posting too frequently may cause users to hide your posts, which will diminish your reach.

Insights

The *Insights* link at the top of your page takes you to the pages that tell you about your audience and how your content performs. There are pages that show what times your audience is active on Facebook, which posts have the most reach and engagement and how often your videos have been viewed. As you go through these pages you'll find an assortment of charts and graphs. There is information about demographics, gender, when they use Facebook, and what types of posts they prefer. These insights should guide what you post, when you post and help you make informed decisions about your content.

Overview shows you what's happening overall — it's self-explanatory and gives you an idea of how your page is trending.

The **Likes** page shows your total page likes — you obviously want this number to grow. It'll also tell you how many have unliked your page, though it won't tell you who. That's probably for the best.

The **Reach** page details individual post reach — that's the number of users your post was served to. It varies based on time of day of your post, type of post and other factors.

Page Views shows you how many have viewed your page and breaks the views down into categories such as section of the page, age, gender and geographic location of the viewer, and the device used to view the page.

Actions on Page tells you how many users have clicked on each element. This is an important number to watch; note the type of post, link, photo, or video, who it's targeting, reach and engagement (likes, comments, shares).

The **Posts** page shows you when most of your fans are online. I found that most of my fans are online around 9:00 p.m., so that's when I post on my Facebook page — your audience may be different and this chart will help you determine the best times to post.

Settings links to the pages that control how the viewers see your page. It's also the place you might add other managers or admins and control who can post to your page and other options.

Go through these options carefully. Under *Visitor Posts,* allow your fans to post to your page. There's really no point to social media if you don't allow your followers to interact with you.

Since I've learned from my own insights that video gets far

more reach than anything else, I know I need to use more video if I want more engagement. Incidentally, the video that got me the most amazing reach was a simple how-to with one of my favorite apps, a recipe program. It's called Paprika and if you're a recipe collector and/or a cook, check it out. Even if it's not exactly related to my work it can still be useful and drive traffic and engagement. Don't be afraid to be creative with video.

Facebook Live

Live video is hot all over and Facebook is no exception. You may have seen the notifications that say "So-and-so is live." Facebook Live automatically alerts your fans that you're live so they can join you. The video will also be available to watch later.

Although the feature debuted on the mobile app, it's now also available on the desktop version. Either way, go to your *Home* feed. You'll see the status field with the "What's on your mind?" placeholder text. Tap *Live* under the status field. A live window will pop up and ask you to describe your video and choose your audience. Tap *Go Live* and you're off and running.

One advantage of Facebook Live is that you can get instant feedback. Viewers can ask questions and indicate that they like your content. Try it — it's a great way to forge a more personal connection.

Twitter

My Twitter Story

I'll start the Twitter section with my own Twitter experience. I posted my first tweet on June 12, 2007. Just for a little perspective, in those days, before the prevalence of smart phones, I often tweeted via text message from my Motorola Razr phone. At that time, few people knew about Twitter, and no one that I knew in real life.

I was fascinated by Twitter and started tweeting more frequently, figuring out how to use it like everyone else. After some time, conversations began to pop up. Through the rest of 2007, the Memphis Twitter community grew, and in the summer of 2008, the city's first *tweetup*, a meeting of Twitter users, was held. We met at a local restaurant. There were eight of us, including my husband and me, and I'm still friends with most of those people.

When our two teenage girls heard about the tweetup, they were concerned. We had carefully taught them about internet safety. That night we heard our *don't-meet-people-you-only-know-from-the-internet* lecture delivered right back to us. At least they listened.

A friend who owned a web development firm soon established a group that met monthly to explore social media and to build a community around this new way of online expression. It was through that community that I developed the skills, relationships, and contacts that have allowed me to build my current business. Thank you, Twitter.

Twitter Basics

Twitter is very different from Facebook in some important ways. On Twitter you'll see a group of short, 280-character messages (only recently expanded from 140), or *tweets,* in your stream. The stream or timeline is the group of messages you see. You can control the sequence of these tweets in your user settings; Twitter will show tweets in reverse chronological order, or, if you choose, the best tweets, chosen by Twitter based on accounts you follow.

Unlike Facebook, connecting on Twitter does not have to be mutual. You choose to follow users whose profile and updates interest you. Follow anyone you like, and they can choose whether or not to follow you back. Unfollow a user by clicking *Unfollow* on the Twitter website or in your app, and, like Facebook, they will not be notified. Many sophisticated Twitter users use mobile or web apps that tell them who has unfollowed them, so it is possible you'll be found out in case that matters. Unfollow judiciously.

There is an option to protect your tweets or make them private so that you must approve any potential followers. The other user will have to request to follow you. Unless you have a specific and compelling reason, don't protect your tweets. Here's why:

- It defeats the purpose of social media and few users will request to follow you. You'll be following far more users than follow you and you lose the benefit of new viewpoints.

- It doesn't work. If you're in a position that depends on confidentiality, it might be that social media isn't for you, as you cannot guarantee those tweets will remain private. Note the dozens of public figures who have set off scandals with unfortunate tweets. Someone will almost always snap a well-timed screenshot that lives on after the tweet has been deleted. Protected tweets give you the illusion of privacy, but don't really protect you.

Twitter is often referred to as a *microblogging* site. Microblogging, as opposed to regular blogging, is an update that may contain a link, an image, or simply text. Other than the character limit, it's not unlike a Facebook status.

Several years ago, food expert Alton Brown felt limited by the character limit, which at the time was 140. He would write wordy tweets on a sticky

> You have 160 characters to convince Twitter that you're worth a follow, so use them wisely.

note, photograph the note and tweet the photo. While it did allow him to post longer updates, he missed the search benefits of plain text. Though some may agree with Brown and view the character limit as a barrier, most Twitter users like it. Nothing will teach you to eliminate extraneous words like a strict character limit. I've become a better, tighter writer since I started using Twitter. The restriction has loosened a bit, as a recent change now excludes URLs, usernames, and images from your character count.

Followers are your community on Twitter and every other social network. Everyone wants more followers. Celebrities often have followers in the millions, sports figures have hundreds of thousands, but the average person has a few hundred. You'll see tweets that offer to sell you followers. Don't do it. First of all, fake followers are worthless. It's better to have 100 engaged followers truly interested in what you have to say that 1000 fake followers. Secondly, it can get you booted from Twitter. It's against their terms of service and if you're caught you can be banned. Not cool.

Your Twitter Profile

Potential new followers will look at your profile to determine whether or not you're worth following, so choose carefully what you post on your bio and profile. While you may use a Twitter app on your computer and mobile devices, it's much easier to set up your profile on the desktop from *Twitter.com.*

Bio —Beginning on the left side of the page, add your bio. You have 160 characters to convince Twitter that you're worth a follow, so use them wisely. I include hashtags in my bio — we'll talk more about hashtags later, but it's a great idea to use them — it's even better if they are keywords.

It's essential to add a link to your website. You can add other links, but complete all available information in the space provided under *Edit Profile.* I also include a link to my book landing page at the very beginning of my bio. You can see my Twitter profile at *Twitter.com/BethGSanders,* or view other prominent profiles to get an idea of the best way to set yours up.

Avatar — Your profile image, which Twitter calls an *avatar* is important. This is different from the avatar, or persona, we discussed in the previous section. By default, when you set up a new account, Twitter assigns you a default image, which has recently changed to a human figure from what used to be an egg, symbolizing the fact that the new account would "hatch" into a bird that tweets. Add your avatar before you send your first tweet. Using the default image signals that you either don't know what you're doing or don't care. Many users refuse to follow any account without a custom avatar.

Username — I use my name (*@bethgsanders*) for my screen name, but you can use a business name or whatever you like if it fits within the allowed characters. Make sure it's easily identifiable and memorable and that it reflects well on you and your business. Don't use a weird combination of characters that will be difficult to recite at a networking event. If you set a custom username for your Facebook page, try to reserve the same name for Twitter. Consistency is your friend.

Cover Image — You can use the same cover image on Twitter as on Facebook, but the size is 1500 pixels wide by 500 pixels high. You cannot link your Twitter cover image, but you can add graphics to your image that point toward a link or CTA. If you don't have a product to offer or a giveaway for lead generation, just use a photo that represents your work or catches the reader's eye.

Likes, Lists, Moments, and Followers — Below the cover image you'll see the number of tweets you've posted, how many users you're following, how many follow you, and your likes, lists, and moments you've created.

Likes shows all the posts from others you've liked, so be cautious with likes. One professional athlete got himself in some serious trouble because he had liked a lot of posts with inappropriate images. You never know when someone might look at your likes, so resist anything controversial or *NSFW* (not safe for work).

Lists are an excellent way to organize those you follow. You can add accounts you follow to lists you create around a topic, geographic area, or any criteria you choose. The lists link on your profile shows how many lists you have been added to.

Moments are groups of tweets you create around a specific event or idea. This link shows the moments you've created. You can see a link to moments at the top left on *Twitter.com*.

How Twitter Lists Work

Once you begin to follow more than a few accounts, you'll

notice it gets more and more difficult to keep up. I follow more than 2000 people, and to read each tweet which would take all day and all night.

Lists make Twitter manageable and help you use it productively. They can be public or private — either way, be careful how you name them, as the names of public lists can be seen. So don't name your public list *Dumb People Who Annoy Me.*

Most Twitter apps support lists so that you can view only the tweets you choose. The desktop app Tweetdeck allows you to organize lists into columns and the Twitter app has an icon that links to your lists.

If you're going to use Twitter for business, use lists as you get started. I waited too long to set them up, and was already following many accounts when they were introduced. It took hours of tedious work to sort through users I follow and add them to lists. Start building your lists from the beginning and add accounts you follow to lists as you go along. You can manage lists from your Twitter app or the Twitter website.

To add a user to a list on the Twitter website, click the gear icon to the left of the *Follow* button and you'll see a dropdown menu with several options, one of which is *Add to or Remove From Lists.* Click that option and your lists will come up, or you can add a new one and add this account to your new list.

Your Follower/Following Ratio

A word about following — don't follow 1000 people at once with the expectation that they will all follow back. Some will, some won't. Keep an eye on your follow/follower ratio. I follow far fewer accounts than follow me. If those two numbers were reversed, my ratio would be poor and I might look like a spammer. Following large groups of users is a tactic spammers often use, on the theory that many people automatically follow back. Follow a few accounts at a time, and give others a chance to catch up and follow you. It's best to have more followers than accounts you follow.

How do you know who to follow back? Check out their profile and look at their last few tweets — are they of interest? Does the user regularly post helpful information? Do they have more followers than accounts they follow? If they look interesting go ahead and follow — you can always unfollow.

Interact on Twitter

Once you get started on Twitter you'll want to connect with others. There are four ways to connect on Twitter:

@Replies • This is when you reply to another account. Let's say you're watching the Oscars. Someone tweets that they hated the movie that won Best Picture. It was your favorite movie, and you want to reply and tell them why you loved it. Click the thought bubble icon under the tweet to reply. Twitter will automatically fill your tweet window with the user's screen name. Depending on their settings the reply will probably be seen by the other user in their notifications. If the user responds, you'll have a conversation. This is the essence of Twitter; these quick, simple conversations with others you wouldn't otherwise interact with.

Likes • It's easy to like a tweet — just click or tap the heart icon under the tweet. This will do a couple of things. It will let the author of the tweet know that you liked it, and save it in your likes column.

Liking a tweet is a great way to save it to read later.

Retweets • This is a bit like sharing your friend's post on Facebook. You do it when you think it's great and want to share it — and when you do, it will probably be interpreted as an endorsement. For this reason, users who work for companies with strict social media policies may be required to add a disclaimer to their profile.

For example, if your favorite sports team tweets about winning a game, you might retweet that and add your own comment to show your enthusiasm. Retweets are great, because both your username and your tweet are shared with others who follow the account that retweets you.

Direct messages • This is a private message that you can send to another Twitter user. Many users don't read their direct messages (DMs), because numerous Twitter accounts send annoying auto-DMs when you follow them. Please, please don't do this. The auto DM will endear you to no one. No matter what anyone tells you, do not sign up for any service that does this automatically. Some users will unfollow; all will be annoyed. Sending a non-spammy DM to another user you are connected to is perfectly fine. Due to changes Twitter has made of late, the other user no longer has to be a follower to receive a DM. Use caution with DMs.

Twitter Apps

If you're serious about Twitter, you'll probably want to download one of the apps I mentioned in the previous section. Most of them are free. Twitter's own official app, aptly named Twitter, is free and available for both Windows and Mac. It's nice if you're a basic user, but once you begin to use lists, you may prefer an app that allows you to display your lists in columns, like Tweetdeck, also owned by Twitter.

Tweetdeck allows you to create columns for the built-in features such as notifications, direct messages and lists. You can also create a column for searches and feeds from other Twitter accounts. I have added my lists to columns; one called *Memphis,* then my notifications, my (private) *fam* list, and *Cardinals* to follow my favorite baseball team. I also have a column for my home feed, which includes folks who aren't on a list, a *Marketing* list and a search for Memphis Weather so I can keep up with our far-too-numerous tornado warnings. While there is a Tweetdeck app for Mac, Windows users are stuck with the web version at *Tweetdeck.Twitter.com.*

There are mobile apps, most notably the official Twitter app, which is free and available for iOS, Android, and Windows phone. The mobile app is easy to use and makes it much simpler to post photos; you may find you prefer mobile.

Hashtags

You've no doubt seen or heard of hashtags — they are everywhere. If there's one thing I get asked to explain time and again, it's hashtags. You see them in the bottom corner of your TV screen, on billboards, t-shirts and posters.

The reason they are so popular is that they are powerful. Think of hashtags as embedded keywords that make the content you post online searchable. For example, on Twitter, if you're watching the World Series and you want to see what others on Twitter are saying about it you can search #WorldSeries. Notice there's no space. Hashtags can only be characters; letters and numbers and are not case sensitive.

Here's a helpful exercise. Brainstorm hashtags you can use to make your social media updates searchable. Here are a few that I use regularly: #SmallBiz #SocialMedia #EmailMarketing #Marketing #Blogging.

Do a Twitter search for your keywords and find the hashtags that relate to them. Store them in a text document so you can quickly copy and paste them into tweets. Hashtags are important on Twitter, Facebook, Instagram, and even LinkedIn, to get your posts noticed by those who don't follow you and may not otherwise see what you're posting. You'll gain more followers as you begin to effectively use hashtags.

Without a hashtag, you're tweeting only to your followers. Add it and you reach anyone who searches that term, and, yes, there are those who do hashtag searches. Outside of lucking into a crazy viral tweet, hashtags are the best way to grow your followers organically.

If you're organizing an event, create a unique hashtag and include it in all communications and advertising. Post it prominently on the day of the event so attendees will see and use it. Many events include the hashtag on the t-shirt design and on signage. This helps build buzz and may even get it trending locally. It also helps attendees meet new people, as they'll notice others using the hashtag. Some conferences even give a prize for tweeting; I once won a cool Bluetooth speaker for being the top tweeter at a conference.

Note how your favorite television shows use hashtags. They do this to build community around their program. Much like the conference or event hashtag, the TV show hashtag draws together users who watch the show, discuss it and build buzz around it.

I know this works. My husband and I didn't watch *Mad Men* when it debuted; it was only after seeing the multitude of tweets that we became curious and next thing we knew we were binge watching to catch up and forever hooked.

Be careful if you appropriate popular hashtags for commercial use. This tactic can work well if done correctly, but if it goes wrong, it can be catastrophic.

Ask DiGiorno Pizza. In September 2014, NFL player Ray Rice was suspended after a video of him punching his then-fiancé Janay Palmer surfaced on social media. In the wake of the scandal that followed, the #WhyIStayed hashtag became popular as women who had been in abusive relationships began to share their reasons for staying with their partners. DiGiorno, without knowing its meaning, tweeted "Because you had pizza" and used the hashtag. Though they meant no harm and there was no evil intent, the company had a backlash on their hands and is frequently used as an example of what can go wrong on Twitter.

Before you use any hashtag, do a search and see what it's about. Search it on Twitter and Google — find its meaning and popular use. Hashtags can do enormous good, but, used thoughtlessly, can be excruciatingly painful.

Automation

If you're tweeting for business and want to maintain your presence, sooner or later you'll have to automate your updates. I don't love automation, but it's necessary and it can be done effectively. Just because you've automated your posts doesn't mean you abandon the platform. Check in a couple of times each day for replies or retweets.

You can automate your posting with apps like Hootsuite or Buffer — both offer free accounts. I've used both, but prefer Buffer as it allows more control over scheduling. Like Hootsuite, they offer a free shortcut for your browser bookmark bar that lets you add content with a click. You can add it via your browser extension settings.

Once you've set up your Buffer account and logged in, add whatever social media accounts you like. Buffer works with Facebook (both pages and profiles), LinkedIn (both profiles and business pages), Twitter, Pinterest, and Instagram. If you're using the free account, you can add one profile per network; the lowest-level paid plan allows a total of ten profiles.

Let's say I'm in my web browser and I happen to see a fascinating post on *BethGSanders.com*. I decide to share it on my social profiles, so I click the Buffer icon I added to my browser. When I click the icon, a dialog box pops up that lets me select which networks I want to post the update to. Buffer will add the post to my queue.

Your *queue* is the list of posts that are scheduled. You can rearrange them with a simple drag and drop. Unlike Hootsuite, Buffer provides the ability to set different schedules for each account, which means I can set my Twitter account to post five times each day, and Facebook only twice. Although it's OK to post to Twitter fives times per day, you certainly wouldn't do that on Facebook or LinkedIn. I also don't repeat posts on Facebook or LinkedIn, while I do repeat popular tweets and all tweets to my original content. Buffer shows you your most popular post on each network, and in the analytics section there is a button to "rebuffer," or repost any update you choose.

One potential downside of social media automation arises

during times of national or international tragedy. You obviously don't want a lighthearted tweet going out at this time. The best thing to do in the wake of a horrific event is to pause your tweets. You can post about the event if you feel you need to, but no one will fault you for going silent. The last thing you want to do is post anything promotional or appear insensitive. This will make you enemies and you'll regret it — there are many examples to prove me right. When in doubt, say nothing.

Trends

On the the Twitter website, you'll see a section called *Trends*. This simply means that many users are talking about a particular topic or hashtag. You'll see the top ten trends in the nation, or your city, depending on how you set your preferences on *Twitter.com*. You can select national trends or tailored trends, which are based on your location and the accounts you follow.

For example, as I write this it's Wednesday and #WednesdayWisdom is trending in the US. Let's say you had a bit of wise advice to dispense. This would be a great day to tweet it with the hashtag, as it's obviously gained a large amount of national attention.

Use trends to see what people are talking about in your city and nationwide. If you can find trends that relate to your business or your audience, join in and use the appropriate hashtag.

Twitter Moments

One feature Twitter has implemented in the last year or so is *moments,* collections of tweets around an occasion or event. There are all kinds of moments from funny memes to serious political issues. To build a moment, choose the tweets you want to include. You can include tweets you've liked, tweets from a specific account, or a hashtag search.

For example, if I wanted to create a moment about spring flowers, I might choose a lovely flower photo from my photo library for the cover image, then add the hashtag search #flowers. Twitter gathers tweets with that hashtag and pulls them into my moment. Once I hit the *Publish* button, my moment is visible to the public, although I could also choose to keep it private.

Build Following Organically

As you build your Twitter following, keep in mind that it's not an overnight process, especially if you build your followers organically. Like most worthwhile endeavors, the easy way is rarely the best way. Take the time to build followers organically and you'll have a far more engaged audience. If you take over an established, successful Twitter account, you still need to review it just to make sure everything reflects positively on you. Whether you're just starting the account or taking over a fledgling Twitter, you'll spend a fair amount of time building and cultivating your audience.

How to Build a Real Following on Twitter

- First, spend time "listening." Acquaint yourself with what your audience is talking about before you jump in. Even if you know your field intimately, invest the time to do some searches on your topic and eavesdrop a bit.
- Retweet others' tweets. When you see something valuable from another account, retweet it and explain why

you think it's worth a read.

- Be helpful. Answer questions, point others to resources, or encourage someone who seems to be having a rough day.
- Post valuable content that helps your readers. Nine of every 10 tweets in your timeless should be others-focused. That means there's only one left that's about you.
- Reply to tweets that interest you and start conversations with other users.
- Take advantage of Twitter at events and conferences. If you're tweeting the official hashtag for the day, you're likely to get others' attention. Interact and engage with them and then introduce yourself in person at the next break.
- Use images to make your tweets more appealing and to increase the click rate. Be sure that you have the right to post the images and aren't violating copyright restrictions. You can find free or inexpensive stock photos online.

Twitter Win

A couple of years ago, Oreo won the Twitter Super Bowl with a well-timed and ingenious tweet that referenced the power outage that occurred during the game. When the lights suddenly went down, Oreo was ready with a tweet featuring a dark background with a light shadow around a cookie and the caption, "You can still dunk in the dark." Sent on the spur of the moment, millions loved it and marveled at Oreo's quick thinking.

It showed a sense of fun and made me want Oreos. Of course, the Super Bowl going dark was not a tragedy, no one was hurt, and it was a light and funny way to have fun with a few moments of darkness. This is how you seize a moment.

Live Tweeting

At some point it's likely you'll be called upon to live tweet. Live tweeting can help you make new contacts, attract followers and forge connections with those you'd otherwise not encounter. You can quickly make a name for yourself if you do it well — providing meaningful content related to the topic at hand, promoting the expertise of speakers and bringing attention to important issues.

I've live tweeted quite a bit through the years, so here are my best live tweeting tips:

- **Don't try to get everything.** That's not the goal. Get the salient points and ideas that your audience will find useful. It's almost impossible to tweet stories or illustrations, so use those times to rest a bit and absorb the speaker's points.
- **Take photos.** Even if you think they aren't exciting, it gives your audience a peek into what it's like to be there. Sometimes photos are truly noteworthy, and sometimes they're just a look into the environment and a chance to see faces and places.
- **Listen and interpret.** Your job is to listen carefully and curate what you're hearing for your audience. It can be tough to paraphrase accurately on the fly, but it gets easier with practice.
- **Use the hashtag** for the event, or invent one if someone hasn't already. The hashtag pulls your tweets together

with others at the event and makes them searchable.

- **Watch and retweet others.** Follow the hashtag in addition to using it. You're not tweeting in a vacuum. If you're at a conference or other event, it's a great way to identify and retweet others who share your interests. And always respond to anyone who has a question or comment.

Instagram

Instagram Stats[19]

- 20 percent of internet users use Instagram
- 400 million monthly active users
- 75 million daily users

Instagram is designed primarily as a mobile app. Though you can view, like and comment on photos on the desktop site, you can't post photos from the web. It's a free download on all mobile platforms. When you first open Instagram, it'll ask you to log in or create an account. Once you're in, it's time to set up your profile. You'll choose a username, and there is space for a bio and a website link. As with Facebook and Twitter, you want to use keywords and hashtags in your bio.

Add a profile photo. If you can keep your profile photos consistent across your social platforms, it will be easy for users to find and recognize you. Across the top of your screen in the app, you'll see your profile photo, the number of posts you've added, your followers and those you are following. Under your name is your bio.

Buttons on the bottom of the screen are *Home* (your feed of posts from those you follow), a search icon, a box with a plus icon that you tap to add a photo, a heart icon that will show you reactions to your posts, and, on the far right, your profile photo. Tap it and it will take you to your profile.

A tap on the plus icon will take you to the photo screen. You'll have a choice between your photo library (existing photos) and *Photo* and *Video,* which let you shoot from within the app. At the lower left of the photo area, there is a pair of arrows; tap them and you'll switch between the front-facing camera and "selfie" view. You'll also see a flash icon at the bottom right of this area.

After you snap the photo, the app will take you to the filter page. Try out each filter to decide which one, if any, you'll use. You can drag your favorites to the left so you can reach them more easily. When you're finished, tap *Next,* which will take you to the post screen. There you'll add your caption, tag friends, add your location, hashtags if you like, and choose which social networks you want to post to. Click *Share* to post and you're done. Since I'm an iPhone user, these instructions are based on the iOS platform. Android layouts may vary slightly, but should not be drastically different.

Once you follow a few users, you'll begin to notice a row of profile photos across the top of the screen. These are Instagram stories. Tap a thumbnail photo and you'll see stories from your friends. If you know you'll be taking a lot of photos in a short time, add the photos to a story instead of annoying your followers with a deluge of images. This feature is similar to Snapchat's stories, and like Snapchat, stories disappear in 24 hours. They are not added to your profile by default, but you can choose to add them.

At first, Instagram was primarily populated by teens and

20-somethings, but now you'll find middle agers, soccer moms, and even a few grandparents. There are also numerous visually-oriented businesses, such as clothing and jewelry designers, travel destinations, and other brands with a strong visual component.

"Instagram delivered ... 58 times more engagement per follower than Facebook, and 120 times more engagement per follower than Twitter."[20]

Instagram is second only to Twitter in the use of hashtags. In fact, because Instagram allows far more characters than Twitter, it's not unusual to see a post with 30 hashtags, the current limit.

How to Build a Following on Instagram

- Before you get started, search for your competitors and others in your field; see what kinds of content they post, and watch how many comments and likes each draws.
- Follow back those who follow you, unless they are obviously spammers. Watch what they post and find ways to engage.
- Use your location no matter where you are. Often Instagram users will search on a particular location, especially if there's a special event. It's just another way to help users find you.
- Try a contest. You can choose a winner randomly or run a caption contest in which you post a photo and the best caption wins. Use your imagination as you think of contest ideas to drive engagement.
- Use hashtags. As we've discussed, hashtags allow your content to be more easily found by those who don't follow

you. You can use up to 30 in each post. Instead of putting them in the caption, add them to the first comment. This is less annoying to the user and you still get the benefit of the hashtags.

- Keep a text file of hashtags on your phone. I use Evernote for this, but you can use a notes app, or any other app that supports plain text. Add your favorite 30 hashtags to a file, where you can easily copy/paste when you post.
- Think creatively. If it's appropriate for your brand, post fun images; dogs are always good.
- Even if you're in a conservative industry like banking, you can still use Instagram. If you have staff members involved in the community, post photos of them in action. Show your customers that you are a good corporate citizen. Highlight staff members and give customers a look behind the scenes. Show staff attending or conducting training.
- Follow accounts that do Instagram well to get inspiration. No one does photography like National Geographic, and their Instagram account is stellar. They post daily photos from around the world and they are spectacular, to which their 47.6 million follows attest. NASA is another winner.

You can convert your personal Instagram to a business profile. Business accounts feature a *Contact* button at the top, a CTA at the bottom, and allow you to add contact information such as email or links. If you decide against the business account, it's easy to switch back to a personal account.

Cool Tip: Display Photos in Twitter's Timeline

Technology companies often don't play well together. This may be why Twitter changed their algorithm so that photos from other sources (such as Instagram) don't display in the timeline. If you post from an external source (like Instagram), you will only see a text link and not the photo itself. Since we know that tweets with images get more engagement, we want our images to be seen, right?

If you use Instagram you can easily share photos to Twitter as you post them to Instagram, however, they will only be displayed as text links. If you want them to display as native photos — photos posted from Twitter — here's how to do it.

There's a free service called *If This, Then That* (IFTTT), at *IFTTT.com*. Set up an account and authorize the Instagram and Twitter channels. You'll find many applets (scripts that do something automatically), but the one you're looking for is called *Post your Instragram pictures as Native Twitter Pictures*. You can do a search for this phrase and you'll find it easily.

Once you find the applet and authorize Twitter and Instagram with your login credentials, all that's left to do is to turn it on. Your photos from Instagram will now display as native Twitter photos. You'll get much more engagement with the images than with a simple text link. Once you turn on the applet, you're good to go — you only have to do it once. You won't need to select the button to post to Twitter in Instagram, as it will automatically post your image.

LinkedIn

As you probably know, LinkedIn is a social network for professionals. The content you'll see there is related to work, and work only.

You do not want to post your family photos or pictures of your dog. It's a popular network and can be especially useful if you're searching for a job. There are paid plans that allow you more freedom in messaging and more analytics about who's viewing your profile. Here are some tips that will help you build a professional profile.

- Use a professional photo. I don't necessarily mean one taken by a professional photographer, but one that looks professional. Skip that cute photo of you with your boyfriend, your mother, or anyone else.

- Use your full name. I shouldn't have to say this. Don't be paranoid about privacy. It's silly to be on LinkedIn as FirstName LastInitial. If you want to be found by potential customers and clients, use your whole name.

- Wear something businesslike. I've seen too many LinkedIn profile photos that show too much skin — or worse, women, boob. Your boobs don't belong in any profile, and especially not on LinkedIn. The only assets you want to display on LinkedIn are those between your ears.

- Post updates to call attention to your profile. I notice more profile views when I post links to articles. You can automate these via Buffer or Hootsuite.

- Add your LinkedIn profile link to your business card. Most profile links follow this format: *LinkedIn.com/in/YourUsername.* Get as close to your real name as possible.

- Connect with others you meet at offline events. Write a personal connection message. Don't depend on LinkedIn's default message. Let the person know how you know them and why you'd like to connect.

- Don't spam the inbox. It's irritating to accept a new connection only to receive an inbox message that tries to sell.
- Fill out all of the available information for your profile and remember to use your keywords.
- Not only can you connect with fellow professionals, you can follow business pages. This may be helpful if there's a company you'd like to work for or do business with, or a brand that puts out interesting information. You can build a business page and add separate showcase pages for products and services. A showcase page is associated with your business page and focuses on a product.

SlideShare

SlideShare Stats[21]

- More than 18 million uploads
- 40 categories
- 500 percent more traffic from business owners than Facebook, Twitter, YouTube, and LinkedIn
- 400,000 new presentations/month.

You may be surprised to see SlideShare on this list. It's not as popular as the other social networks we're discussing, and not everyone is familiar with it, but I think it's important to know about. I include SlideShare because it's owned by LinkedIn and there are those who have built a strong following on the platform.

Most people think about SlideShare for presentations, but it's not only for slide decks. You can create and adapt content for SlideShare. Try it with a blog post: boil it down to a presentation format with graphics and post it on Slidehare with all of the appropriate tags, which will be your … you guessed it … keywords.

You can upload a Microsoft PowerPoint file, but if you're an Apple Keynote user, you'll have to export your file to a *Portable Document Format (PDF)* file. Any file you can save or export as a PDF can be uploaded to SlideShare, so I hope you are already thinking of some content you can convert to a SlideShare-able format.

Optimize SlideShare

- Use keywords in your description (fill it out fully).
- Make your first slide eye catching and engaging.
- Audience: professionals. Prepare accordingly.
- Fill out your profile with links to other social profiles and especially your website. Add keywords to your bio. By default the files you upload will be embeddable so that viewers can add them to their own websites. It's best to make your files embeddable, but whether or not they are available for download is up to you.

SlideShare is an underutilized resource for content discovery. The analytics are surprisingly robust and show you where your viewers come from, who they are, and much more. Use SlideShare especially if you produce presentations, but also if you have other content that can be adapted to its format.

Snapchat

Snapchat is an exclusively mobile app, a favorite of teens and 20-somethings, but has not yet caught on quite as much with the older crowd. Perhaps that is because it's much harder to find other users on Snapchat and the interface is not particularly intuitive.

Snapchat has only recently added a search feature; you can now look up other users by their username, or do a keyword search to view live stories. You can also add another user with their *snapcode,* a unique coded image generated when you set up your account.

Many of Snapchat's users are *digital natives,* that is, persons who were born or brought up during the age of digital technology and familiar with computers and the internet from an early age. Snapchat's interface brings frustration to those who struggle with technology, whatever their chronological age.

There are several ways to add friends to Snapchat; you can search the contacts on your phone, or find another user by entering their user name if you know the exact name. You can also add friends who are nearby, thanks to GPS integration. The most unique way to add a friend is to use a *snapcode.* The snapcode is a special code you create in the app — it's a rounded square with a yellow background and a seemingly random arrangement of dots, which actually make up a unique code. The icon you choose for your profile appears in the center of the code. You may have seen snapcodes as profile photos on other social networks. When you see a snapcode, just take a photo of it with your phone. When you open the image in Snapchat it automatically scans the code and adds the user to your friends list.

The idea behind Snapchat is temporary content; your posts disappear after 24 hours. Although it can no longer be viewed in the app after that period, there is no guarantee that it is truly gone, so post carefully. There is no need for perfect content since it is temporary. It's more important to be quick and current than to be perfect.

Snap Tips

- Snap at an event or show your staff doing cool things.
- Take a casual video poll around the office on a fun subject: pets, kids, pet peeves, and other light and timely topics.
- Talk directly to your customers about something that will be important to them; perhaps a noncontroversial cause.
- Show your lighter side. If you want to get a bit creative it's OK; you can also cover heavier topics where appropriate.

Food Network does a tremendous job with Snapchat, with cooking tips, recipes and appetizing photos. Snapchat's *Discover* section features brands' content, and again National Geographic is a winner. You'll see beautiful photos that will take you to riveting nature and animal stories with just an upward swipe.

As a business you can advertise on Snapchat if it fits your demographic — but you'd better have a large budget. If your budget is more modest, you can still make your presence known on Snapchat, as it costs nothing to create a *geofilter*. A geofilter is a graphic that users can add to their images when they are at or near your location. It might identify their town, or a venue, say for a rock concert or other large event. If you're a brick and mortar business, you can easily make your own geofilter and add it at no charge.

To build your geofilter, create a graphic with a transparent background and upload it in .png format. You'll have to use a vector graphic application such as Adobe Illustrator to create the image, or ask a graphic designer to do it for you. Submit the image to Snapchat via their website. You will specify a geofence, an area inside of which you want the filter to be active. It's generally about a one-block radius for a business location. When a user is at or near you they can swipe left to find and apply your geofilter. Snapchatters know this and look for geofilters when they post. It takes a week or so to get approval.

The best content for Snapchat is quick videos and fun, attractive images that draw attention immediately. It's fast-paced and energetic. Like Instagram, you can add your snaps to stories that your friends can view. The images will cycle through automatically, but you can swipe right to go quickly to the next. This feature was first created by Snapchat and has now been copied on both Instagram and Facebook.

YouTube

YouTube Stats[22]

- 1 billion (with a *b*) users
- 400 hours of video uploaded to YouTube every minute
- Second largest search engine, after Google[23]

Chances are you've spent some time on YouTube. Whether you're wasting time when you should be working or learning a new skill, you can find most anything. As you probably know, YouTube is owned by Google, which makes it an important place to have a presence if you want to get found online.

Earlier I mentioned the one-and-a-half hour YouTube video that demonstrated how to reupholster a chair. You may remember, the video was extremely detailed, and when it was over, I felt as if I could do the job. The video was posted by a company called Sailrite that sells fabrics and other upholstery supplies. Instead of just screaming "Buy our products!" Sailrite made an interesting and useful video that shows how their products are used and makes you want to buy them.

As a business, it's wise to add YouTube to your marketing strategy. Set up a channel, add your branding and a link to your website. YouTube allows you to place links and "cards" within your videos that encourage viewers to go to your website or learn more about the topic of the video. Users can subscribe to your channel to get notifications when you post new content.

YouTube's Video Manager allows you to edit your video and add a description. Fill the description out completely and use your keywords in both the description and the tags. YouTube offers myriad settings and tools that enhance your video and audio. There is also royalty-free music you can use in your videos, which keeps you from violating copyright laws. YouTube will remove your video if you use music that you do not hold a license to use.

As you plan your online strategies, consider how you can use video to draw users in. Whether it's how-tos, a peek behind the scenes, or testimonials, most businesses can find a way to capture a video audience. As an example, Goulet Pens' YouTube channel is fun. You can find them by searching their name. They specialize in fountain pens in various price ranges, and offer videos that appeal to pen enthusiasts. Goulet uses YouTube to educate their customers, which is one of their stated missions. Yes, it's a niche market, but it's very successful for them.

Consider what sort of video content you can generate that will highlight your business in a unique way. Teach your viewers to do something, or just make it fun. It's OK to show your human side.

Vimeo

Vimeo Stats[24]

- Monthly viewers: 170 million
- Cleaner interface for embedded video
- No ads

I've included Vimeo because it's a slightly different kind of video site than YouTube. I use both for different reasons and this is something you may want to do if you produce many videos.

With no ads, Vimeo's interface and embedded videos look much cleaner. When I create videos, I upload them to both Vimeo and YouTube. I use YouTube for the distribution and search advantage; Vimeo for the appearance. When I embed the videos on my website I do so from Vimeo. It's a bit of extra trouble to upload the same video to two different platforms, but the embeds look much cleaner and I don't lose the Google advantage of YouTube. Like YouTube, Vimeo allows you to add descriptions and tags. Write your descriptions and decide on your tags before you upload, then you can copy and paste on both sites. Both sites generally provide tag suggestions as well.

One of the reasons Vimeo's video embeds are so much more attractive is the ability to control the appearance. I like to use the blue from my logo as it blends nicely with the rest of my website; this ability to do this is a paid feature. You can also choose what text you display, such as the title, channel name, and whether or not to show your profile photo on the video embed.

Wrapup

We've come to the end of the social networks I chose to feature. Although there are others, if you can effectively use these you'll have a great start online.

There's a lot of talk about privacy these days. The truth is, we really aren't guaranteed any sort of privacy. If you want to keep it private, don't post it online. Remember:

- No matter how few followers you have, you can't hide anything you post on the internet.
- Deleting isn't always deleting. Screenshots of deleted social media updates get publicized all the time. There is no deniability online.
- Choose the social networks that work best for you.
- Always put your best foot forward.
- Decide how many networks you can realistically do well, and choose those. You don't have to be everywhere.

7

Email Marketing

E mail marketing is perhaps one of the most powerful tools for any organization or businessperson. If done thoughtfully, it can help generate and nurture leads while you sleep. Most small organizations use email in some form; few of them use it effectively.

We must consider email marketing not in isolation, but in context of an overall plan. It's not as simple as sending an "email blast" (please don't call it that) to your customers. There's a right way to go about gathering email addresses to build your list, and knowing where on your website to route them is key.

If you're not already capturing email addresses on your website, start now. I mean now. I confess I didn't follow my own advice on this. I'd advise clients to build their lists, and I never built a website for a client that didn't include an email capture, but I waited far too long to begin building my own list. Don't be like me. Start building your list yesterday. You're welcome.

Email marketing is successful because it's the closest to one-on-one communication you can get with your audience. Everything else — social media, your blog, your website, even print — is a one-to-many relationship.

You can think of your email subscribers as *warm leads*. A warm lead, as opposed to a cold lead, is someone who at least knows who you are and has indicated that they have at least some degree of affinity for you. A reader who has opted in to your email list is a warm lead.

Email has proven effective in *lead nurturing;* that is, guiding your prospect through the buying process through a series of automated emails. For example, I may see you on Facebook or another social network, or I might visit your website. On your site you presumably have a signup form, and a free giveaway that appeals to me. I sign up, and receive a welcome email.

Over the next few weeks I receive regular emails from you that are designed to take me from tire kicking to giving you my credit card information. Each interaction is part of the relationship building process that make me comfortable giving you my money.

When you're in your customers' inbox, they are looking at your email and nothing else. It's as if you've been invited to their living room as a guest. For that sliver of time, you, and only you, have their full attention. We're going to talk about how to make the most of that invitation and how not to become an unwelcome guest.

Now that you've realized it's time to get rolling with email marketing, how do you get started?

Choose a Provider

Many time I've been asked, "Why can't I just use my business email account to send my newsletter?" It's an excellent question. The reason this won't work is that no regular email client will allow you to send bulk emails due to spam regulations. You'd have to send the emails in batches, which takes far too long, and, more importantly, you lose the analytics, list management, and other important features your email provider gives you.

First you'll need to choose an email provider. There are numerous email marketing services, and they vary on price and features. Some have free tiers (such as MailChimp), and all have different pricing structures, so it pays to spend some time determining which best fits your needs and budget.

Here are some of the major email providers. This is by no means a complete list, but I've used all of these services and can recommend any of them depending on your needs.

- Constant Contact (the first well-known service)
- Vertical Response
- Emma
- MailChimp
- Campaign Monitor (the very best if you're into detailed stats)
- Active Campaign (what I currently use)

If you use a customer relationship management (CRM) system, such as SugarCRM or Salesforce to manage leads and accounts, choose an email service that can integrate with it to save you time and trouble.

If you do not have a CRM, explore these and other providers and do your due diligence. (Although I have used and recommend all of these services, I have no relationship other than that of a satisfied customer.)

> **Email has proven effective in lead nurturing ... guiding your prospect through the buying process.**

Many beginners start with MailChimp for its ease of use and free plan. Designed for the less technically inclined, it's one of the most user-friendly services, and one of the only ones with a free tier. You'll have to start paying when your subscribers top 2000, and, unless you are wildly popular, that could be a while.

Once you've chosen your provider and set up your account, you can add your first list. Depending on your offerings, you may need more than one list.

List Building

You'll get many of your users via a signup form generated by your email provider and embedded on your website. These forms have fields for name, email address, and other information you need to capture. When the user enters their information, the form communicates with your email provider and automatically adds the contact to your list.

As you build your form, consider the copy carefully. The headline should clearly reflect the benefit. Use simple language and a large, easy-to-read font. Don't get clever, just be clear. Make your form fields large and easy to read and use as few as you can get away with. For initial signup, name and email address should suffice.

When designing your form, be sure the text has a high contrast against the background. I like to place forms at both the top and bottom of the page, and, if it's a very long page, I'll put one in the middle as well.

Depending on which part of the page the form appears on, you may or may not need much copy. A form at the bottom of a long landing page may only need, "I'm Ready — Sign Me Up."

Many studies have shown that the more information you try to collect, the greater the resistance to signing up. Capture only what you really need, rather than risk losing a potential customer with a form that's too involved.

The form should remind the user what they're getting into. Will they get a weekly newsletter, access to a free giveaway, or special discounts? Be clear about their benefit and why they should sign up. Use a compelling offer or giveaway as few readers will be excited about your newsletter.

Say the background of your email signup box is a nice blue with white text. The CTA button might be a bright orange, which makes it stand out from the rest of the box. While it's esthetically pleasing to make the button blend with your color scheme, if you're looking for conversions, or sales, the button should pop. For best results, it's better if the button is a bright color and contrasts with its surroundings.

Button copy is critical. This is sometimes called *microcopy,* but there is nothing small about its importance. *YES! Sign Me Up For the Minicourse* conveys much more value than the default *Submit* copy, which you should never use. Always customize your button copy to your offer. *Yes! Send Me the Ebook!* is much more compelling than

Submit, as you remind the reader of what they will receive.

It's also a good idea to include a statement that you will not sell or rent their information to anyone — this inspires trust and makes the user more comfortable with handing over their email address.

Most email providers allow for double opt in, which is considered a best practice. Here's how it works. The user enters their information in the form. They then receive an email asking that they click a link to confirm their subscription. While it may seem cumbersome, one advantage is that you'll end up only with subscribers who care about hearing from you. A disadvantage is that sometimes the confirmation emails can be missed or even land in the spam folder, so the user doesn't get added due to lack of confirmation. It's up to you to decide what's best for your readers.

Lead Magnets

How do you get people to give you their email addresses? Spammers have made that a difficult proposition. Few of us give our real email addresses so readily for a newsletter that's unproven.

This is why you need a *lead magnet.* A lead magnet is an ethical bribe. You coax the user to give you their email address in exchange for something of value. Think about what it would take for you to give your email address to a complete stranger you've only met on the internet.

Make your lead magnet irresistible. It should be so good that you could sell it if you wanted to. Don't worry about giving away too much at this point; it's entirely worth it to grow an excellent list.

You've probably downloaded a lead magnet, but just in case you haven't, here's how it works. You're browsing your favorite website when you notice a headline that says *FREE Ebook That Will Teach You How to Build a Rocket.* Cool. You've always wanted to learn to build a rocket, so you enter your name, email address and click the button to complete the transaction.

Your lead magnet can be a free guide, tipsheet, cheatsheet, ebook, or any other piece of content that you produce. It should be relevant enough to what you do to draw the right audience, and it should be good enough to be of obvious benefit. For example, I offer a seven-week email course on the material in this book as a lead magnet.

After you've entered your email address, and perhaps your name, you may receive an email with a download link for the free ebook, or, as is the case on my site, you are redirected to a special *Thank You* page that includes the download link and other opportunities to connect. Your name and email address get added to the site owner's email provider and you begin receiving their messages.

I include the download link, social media follow buttons, a few recent blog posts, and other features on my *Thank You* page to encourage the new contact to engage on my website.

Creating Your Lead Magnet

If you created your avatar back in the first chapter, this will not be difficult. As much as is possible, you know what your audience thinks, feels, wants, and needs; now all you have to do is give it to them. We all love to get something free and if you can give them free content that solves their problems and meets their needs, you've made a loyal friend.

Let's say you own a garden store. You're collecting email addresses so that you can drive sales and visits to your store. Of course you have opportunities to sign up inside your physical location, but how might you draw signups online?

If I were the owner, I'd create a one- or two-page guide that gives advice on what flowers do best in your climate zone. You might call it *The 10 Best Flowers for Your Yard*. Or, maybe you can help conquer every gardener's nemesis with *25 Ways to Get Rid of Weeds*. When a wannabe green thumb sees this featured on your website, they will want this guide enough to give you their email address.

To the reader, the quality of your lead magnet will reflect the quality of your work. The format will vary according to your topic. If your audience is engineers, for example, you may include drawings and you must be sure to use a clean, readable font to communicate technical information.

A light-hearted topic like gardening lends itself to more color and maybe a fun font used sparingly. No matter what the format, ensure that your grammar and punctuation are correct and your copy is typo free. No writer is immune to the need for a second set of eyeballs on their work, so ask a friend or colleague to proofread and provide feedback.

I use Adobe InDesign to create my lead magnets, but if you don't have access to professional design software, Microsoft Word will work, as will Apple's iWork suite, or (free) Google Docs. The only requirement is that the application you use must be able to export to a PDF.

If you've ever prepared a great-looking document and noticed it looks terrible on someone else's computer, you'll appreciate the PDF file. It embeds your fonts and images and keeps your document intact. This is the standard format for lead magnets as most users have access to the free Adobe Reader that opens these files.

Once your lead magnet is created, proofread, and exported to PDF you'll want to add it to your website. Each file or document you upload to your website has its own URL. This is the URL you'll use for your download link. When the user clicks on the link, it takes them directly to the PDF, which their web browser will download.

Know the Laws

As you build your email list, it's important to acquaint yourself with the laws that apply to email marketing. It's particularly important to understand the CAN-SPAM Act[25] and what it means for your marketing program. Email lists are *permission based,* which means you may only email users who have opted in to your list. This means you do not go to a conference, collect business cards and add your new contacts to your list unless they have specifically requested that you do so.

While you may think it's worth it to have a larger list, this can bite you in a couple of ways. First, your analytics won't be meaningful. Those who aren't truly interested in hearing from you aren't going to open your emails, so your open rate may be skewed.

Those you add without asking may — and have every right to — report you for spam. It doesn't take many spam reports to begin to affect your *deliverability,* or the number of users who actually receive your email. All email programs, or clients, have spam filtering. Gmail is especially noted for their excellent and rigorous spam filtering. Don't risk landing in your readers' spam folder.

You may be tempted to shortcut the list building process by

buying or renting a list. Don't. You will not get the results you hope for. The only way to build an engaged, effective list is to do it the hard way — by asking for signups and offering quality content in return. Always, always ask permission.

Although I urge you to review CAN-SPAM it in its entirety, here are a few salient points:

- You are subject to penalties of up to $16,000 for each email sent to a user after that user has opted out.
- Don't use false or misleading header information.
- Tell recipients where you're located (a physical address). You can use a post office box if you work from home.
- Tell recipients how to opt out of receiving future email.
- Honor opt-out requests within 10 business days.
- The rest can be found on the Federal Trade Commission (FTC) website, *https://www.ftc.gov/tips-advice/ business-center/guidance/can-spam-act-compliance-guide-business.*

The FTC is serious about this and, though you may get away with it for a while, you can face serious consequences and heavy fines if you run afoul of CAN-SPAM.

Email Marketing Strategy

Set Goals

Before you begin your email marketing campaign, decide what you want to accomplish. What is your goal?

- Sales?
- Lead nurturing?

- Information/educa-
  tion?

> Marketing Sherpa ... reports that personalized subject lines increase email open rates by 29.3 percent.

Once your goals are in place, consider the best strategies to meet them. If you sell large-ticket items, lead nurturing will be particularly important. Typically, the higher the price, the longer the sales process. Most of us would not buy a car or a house on impulse as we might a new gadget or a fun shade of lipstick. Your product will determine your goals and selling process.

Email has an excellent track record as a lead nurturing methodology, especially when you automate the messages. You can set up an entire sequence that takes the buyer through the buying process email by email. Messages may be triggered by user actions, such as a purchase or an abandoned shopping cart.

A sales email is much more immediate. The brands I like are welcome in my inbox to show me what's on sale and what's new. I love clothing and fashion and look forward to emails from high-end women's stores that show the latest accessories and outfits, even when I'm not looking to buy.

Types of Email

Will you send a newsletter with industry articles and news? A weekly coupon or sale special? Hints, tips and tricks? I get many newsletters and they take different forms.

In the span of a couple of hours one day, I received the following in my inbox:

- A message from a domain name registrar telling me

about a limited-time special.

- A holiday email with a "gift" of links to their articles and a call to action (schedule a time to talk. I didn't).
- An email from CoSchedule (an editorial calendar platform) that alerted me about new content on their website.
- An informational message from Yoast (they make the leading SEO solution for WordPress) which contained short teasers with links to their content.

Each of these emails falls into one of these categories:

- **Transactional:** These messages thank the customer for purchasing or deliver the promised product or lead magnet. They may be simple thank-you notes with a download link.
- **E-Newsletters:** E-newsletters inform and educate. They may contain entire articles or teaser paragraphs that link to a blog or website. They should contain a call to action, but primarily consist of news and articles.
- **Promotional:** These emails tell you your favorite sweater is 50 percent off with this special code and make you want to click *buy* quickly.
- **Informational:** Emails that inform you about upcoming events or industry news. They may contain registration links and CTAs.

Some organizations include entire articles in their emails, others send titles and brief descriptions with links to their website or blog. There are advantages and disadvantages for each format; test, test, test to determine which works best for your needs.

How Often Should I Email?

While it's a good idea to have a consistent schedule, the frequency is between you and your audience. You might survey your list to ask what they prefer, or just start with a weekly delivery.

I receive some emails that come weekly, and even one that is sent daily, although that's the exception. The more promotional your newsletter is, the less frequently you want to send it in most cases — although if you're offering regular discounts or sales you may be able to pull off sending it more often. Once you decide on a schedule, stick to it — it's better to send less frequently and consistently than set the bar too high and stress yourself out or be unable to meet the schedule.

Remember that you're in your reader's virtual living room and respect the space. Don't be overly promotional or abuse their hospitality. If done well, email can help you nurture leads and relationships to build sales. Always give the reader something helpful and high quality.

Email Design Considerations

There are two directions you can go when it comes to email design; plain text or HTML. An HTML email contains images, formatting and generally buttons instead of plain text links. Remember, in the website chapter we learned that HTML is how web pages are built and emails can be built this way as well.

Plain text emails are gaining popularity because they are less affected by email clients' filters. They look more like an email between friends or colleagues and, as a result, are more deliverable.

According to a study by Hubspot, an inbound marketing and sales platform that helps companies attract visitors, plain text emails perform better than their HTML counterparts.[26]

The plain text format forces you to be creative with your copy as it's all you have. It must be tight, well written and it has to sparkle. Spend the time you would normally use for design for an HTML email on your copy. If you're not confident in your ability to write it, you may wish to hire a copywriter.

Emails formatted in HTML are more complicated to create and to adapt to smaller mobile screens. According to MarketingLand,

> "... 66 percent of all email in the U.S. is now opened/ read on smartphones or tablets and 34 percent is viewed on a desktop. The mobile breakdown is as follows: 49.5 percent of email opens were on a smartphone, 16.8 on a tablet. Of the 66 percent of mobile opens, 58 percent happened on an Apple device; seven percent were on Android devices."[27]

It's clear from these results that an email that looks good on mobile devices is a necessity, however many marketers are not there yet. I get scores of newsletters and there are still too many that aren't mobile friendly. This is a colossal mistake.

Most email providers offer *responsive,* or mobile friendly templates, so there's no excuse for sending an email that isn't mobile compatible. Use a mobile-friendly template so that your content fits and resizes gracefully as the screen size decreases. You can check this easily in previews and by sending a test email to your phone. If you ignore mobile, you're alienating 66 percent of your audience. I don't know about you, but I cannot afford to do that.

Depending on your provider, email design is relatively easy. It's generally as simple as drag and drop to lay out a well-designed email. You can add images, text blocks, buttons, and other elements. You can also add HTML code if you're so inclined. Let's break down the parts of an email and talk about each one.

The **pre-header,** just above the header, gives the reader an idea of what's in the email — a sort of table of contents, and a link to view the email in a browser.

Next is the **header** section, which usually contains a company logo or wordmark. Just like your website, the convention is that your header image links to your home page. If it looks like your website, the reader will recognize and easily identify it as yours. I keep the header small and just use my logo, linked to my home page.

After the header, the first item is generally your **lead story** or feature; the most important or most prominent content. You'll have to decide whether it's a teaser with a link to your website or if you wish to include the entire story. There's a case to be made for both, and which format you use depends on your audience.

Pay close attention to your subject line. It can make or break your open rate. Much has been written about how to construct a compelling subject line, and studies have been done that support the idea of personalization, that is, using the reader's name or other information, such as location or interests, in the subject line.

Tips for Subject Lines

- **Personalize.** Your email provider should make it easy to personalize your emails. Marketing Sherpa, a research institute that studies effective marketing practices, reports that personalized subject lines increase email open rates by 29.3 percent. "Transaction rates were 49 percent higher (0.09 percent compared to 0.06 percent) and revenue per email was 73 percent higher ($0.15 compared to $0.08) with personalization, according to Experian."[28] Most email providers include merge tags to help you incorporate personalization in your subject line and/or the body of your email.

- Make your **subject line** short and to the point, preferably 50 characters or fewer. You can add emoji to the subject line, however, not all email will clients render them correctly. They can help catch the reader's eye if displayed correctly, but be sure to preview your subject line in different email clients.

- Most email providers include some form of **testing** prior to scheduling or sending your email. It's common to test subject lines; half of your list is delivered one subject line, the other half an alternate line and the difference in open rate is measured. This is called *A/B testing*. You can test variables such as send time, from name, content, and subject line with most email services. Test only one of these variables at a time.

Although most recommend at least a 5000-member list for statistically valid results, there's no reason you can't test with your own list whatever the size. Even if the results are not statistically valid by mathematical standards, you can still spot trends or tendencies in the data and glean information about your customers that can help you make better decisions.

Email Essentials

- **Header image** and branding that links to your website.
- **A call to action** — ask the reader to do something.
- An easy-to-find **unsubscribe link** (usually added by your provider) as required by CAN-SPAM.
- **Social follow buttons** — usually in the footer.
- **Social share/forward links** that encourage your reader to forward to a friend or share on social media. These are different from the social follow links, as they enable the reader to share your content. You need both.
- **Your physical address** (required by CAN-SPAM). I use a post office box as I work from my home office and am not about to use my home address.
- **From email address.** This should be an email address from your domain — *YourWebsite.com.*
- **Reply to address.** This can be the same email address as the from address unless you prefer to route responses to a different email address.
- If you're publishing an HTML newsletter, you'll also need a **plain-text** version, which most providers generate automatically.
- **Read online link** — in case the email client doesn't render the email accurately (many don't). This is usually at the top of the email.
- At least one **image** unless you're using plain text, for tracking purposes. Most email providers track email opens by monitoring whether or not images are opened.

- **Alt tags** on images so that readers who don't display images in their email client can at least get an idea of the missing visual. The alt tag should describe the image.
- **Subject line.** Carefully chosen and 50 characters or fewer.
- A **statement** that tells the reader why they are receiving the email and reminds them that they signed up so they don't send you to spam.

Advanced Email Strategies

List Segmentation

List segmentation is a way of targeting list members based on specific variables such as opens, geography, buying behavior and other factors. Most email software allows you to group and target list members based on these or similar. MailChimp found open rates 14.32 percent higher than non-segmented campaigns when they studied senders who segment vs. senders who do not. They also discovered click rates 85.74 percent higher than non-segmented campaigns and unsubscribe rates 9.92 percent lower than non-segmented campaigns.[29] It's clear that users respond to content that is more closely targeted to their preferences and behaviors.

Most major email marketing services offer list segmentation. For example, you might hold a local event and target only list members within a certain geographic radius. Rather than annoy those who live far away, you can send the message only to members in the area.

Or you may have a new product you know will appeal to purchasers of another product — you can segment your list based on previous purchases. The more specific the message is to the reader's preferences and desires, the more likely they are to welcome the message and to engage.

Email Automation

Most email providers will provide automation capabilities. MailChimp offers numerous templates available online for lead nurturing emails, as does Active Campaign. You can set up an automation, for example, to welcome your new subscribers to the list and deliver your lead magnet. You'll be able to control the look and copy for this email, so make it consistent with your brand and encourage further engagement.

You can set up an email schedule triggered by elapsed time or by behavior. For example, I often resend my email newsletter only to those who didn't open it the first time. A few open it the second time; the open rate is usually about the same as the original email.

Automated emails are often used for lead nurturing. According to a report from Forrester, one of the most influential research and advisory firms in the world, nurtured leads produce, on average, a 20 percent increase in sales opportunities. Furthermore, the research reveals that companies that excel at lead nurturing generate 50 percent more sales at a 33 percent lower cost.[30]

You can trigger an email to be sent by just about anything you can think of — a purchase, abandoned shopping cart, click, and many more. A smart way to use email for lead nurturing is to reward your best customers. Target by their buying behavior and send them exclusive perks; perhaps they get to shop the sale one day early, earn an additional discount, or receive a gift with purchase. Consider what action you want from your reader and reward those who take that action. Lead nurturing strategies include targeted follow-up messages, personalization, and others.

Quick follow-up is key. According to Hubspot, the odds of a lead entering the sales process, or becoming qualified, are 21 times greater when contacted within five minutes versus 30 minutes after an inbound lead converts on your website.[31] This kind of quick, effective followup is easy to do with automation.

According to the *Lead Generation Marketing Effectiveness Study,* 68 percent of successful marketers cite lead scoring based on content and engagement as the most effective tactic for improving revenue contribution from lead nurturing.[32] *Lead scoring* is a rating of the quality of a lead based on their engagement. You can create segments based on lead scores and send to only higher-scoring segments. When you set up your lead nurturing program, invest the time to prepare excellent copy for each email.

Think through the conversion journey — what do prospects need to know about you and your product or service before they're ready to buy? Consider how you can take them through the process smoothly, establish trust, and help them feel good about handing over their money. Spend time editing your copy and images, if you use them, and carefully consider your call to action.

Even if you're not selling, it's easy to evaluate your progress and effectiveness; that's one thing all of the major email providers excel at. You'll know instantly who's opening your message, who's clicking and what they are clicking. Re-evaluate and modify your CTAs based on these numbers. Your provider will include a dashboard that shows you analytics data on the various benchmarks. We'll go into more detail on the analytics in our ROI chapter.

Email marketing is an essential part of your online marketing, and is most effective when it's part of a well-designed strategy that encompasses everything you do online.

Is It Working?

For many of us, measuring results is one of the least fun parts of our work. It's not particularly creative, and let's face it, it can be a little scary. It's a bit like getting on the scale after you've been on a new diet and exercise program for a couple of weeks. You want to measure your progress, but you're nervous about the number. Or maybe you've taken a class. You know you've studied hard and have a good grasp of the material, but you won't breathe easy until you see that letter *A*.

As is the case with everything else in business, the time will come when you need to show your return on investment (ROI). There are many ways to measure ROI, from tracking replies and retweets to monitoring Google Analytics data.

Services such as Hootsuite and Buffer will give you analytics on your social media updates, such as retweets, likes, and potential reach. There are also paid services that allow you more detailed analytics, but they can get expensive.

Google Analytics is your friend. It's free and if you put your mind to it, you can get much of the information you need to make the best decisions.

Rather than letting measurement remind you of that dreaded step onto the scale, let's think of our ROI measurement in a slightly different way. Imagine you're trying to find your way to an exciting event in an unfamiliar city and you make a wrong turn. When your GPS starts shouting (doesn't it always seem they are shouting?) "Recalculating!" it's telling you, "Look, you're going the wrong way, but I have data you don't have and I can get you on track so that you end up where you want to go." This is how I prefer to think of analytics data and I hope you will too.

Email Analytics

You set goals when you started, didn't you?

Your email provider will show you detailed reports that tell you quite a bit about the effectiveness of your efforts. If you're selling, you'll obviously measure conversions — sales and revenue. This is, of course, the bottom-line measuring stick for the effectiveness of your email program.

The report will show you *bounces* — both soft and hard. A bounce means the email did not go to the intended recipient. A *soft bounce* occurs when the user's email is temporarily offline — the provider will usually try to resend. It could be that their email server is down, or, more commonly, their mailbox is full.

A *hard bounce* happens when the email is no longer in existence; for example if you leave Company A to work for Company B, your Company A email address will stop working. Or if you change internet service providers and your email changes, a hard bounce will result. The service will track both types of bounces and purge addresses that hard bounce repeatedly. This helps maintain your deliverability and keeps your analytics more accurate.

You'll also track the time of day that your message is opened and how many times it's opened. This can help you determine the best send times, although most providers have the capacity to send automatically at the best time for you based on your list's history. You can also evaluate the effectiveness of your subject lines — are they enticing the reader to open your email or do you land in the trash? Benchmarks vary widely across industries, so check the average click rate, open rate, and other statistics against those in your industry. You email provider should have these figures readily available; if not, a quick Google search will help you find what you're looking for.

To track conversions, you'll use the *Thank You* page on your website. As this page is not linked to another page or on your menu, the only way a user would find it is to complete the conversion. As you examine your analytics, see in your Google Analytics data the number of times users have accessed this page, divide it by the number of visitors to your landing page and you'll have your conversion rate.

Conversion Troubleshooting: Where to Look

If you're not pleased with your conversion rate, it's time to troubleshoot. Let's trace our users' path through our buying process and see where the breakdown may be.

Imagine the user received an email from you with a CTA. In the best case, the user reads your copy, clicks on the CTA, which takes them to the landing page. They read the landing page copy and click the *Buy* button. They complete the checkout process and are redirected to your *Thank You* page. Google Analytics records the visit to this page.

In situation number two, your initial CTA doesn't compel them to do anything, so nothing happens, no click, no sale. Or, perhaps, they click the CTA, arrive at the landing page and stop. That's a signal to re-evaluate your landing page copy, layout, and images. Are the images aspirational? Do they draw the eye to the copy?

What if your reader clicks the CTA through to the landing page, then clicks the *Buy* button but doesn't complete the sale? Is your checkout process easy to navigate? Are the checkout pages secure, so that the user feels confident as they enter their financial information?

Here is another way to visualize this troubleshooting process.

- CTA Click > User Arrives on Landing Page > Clicks Buy Button > Checkout > Buy >Arrives at *Thank You* Page. This is a conversion. Happiness everywhere.

- No Link Click. Sadness all around.

- CTA > Link Click > User Arrives at landing page > Goes no further

- CTA > Click > Landing Page > Buy. The user clicked through to buy, but didn't complete the transaction for some reason.

If you're more visual, this table may help. Study this process and incorporate it into your reporting to help you find the weak spots.

Begin	Response	Result	Action	Result	Check
CTA	Click	Landing Page	Click Buy Button	Sale Completed	All is well!
CTA	No Click				Check CTA
CTA	Click	Landing Page	No Click		Check Landing Page
CTA	Click	Landing Page	Click Buy Button	Sale Not Completed	Check Checkout Process
© Beth G. Sanders					

Social Media Analytics

Measuring social media effectiveness is a little like trying to pin down a cloud. So much of what makes it work is relationship building, and how on earth do you track that?

The Buffer Blog suggests seven social media engagement metrics to help you measure your effectiveness.

For audience size, Buffer recommends monitoring:[33]

- Audience growth rate.
- New follower rate.
- Follower/following ratio.

And for audience engagement:

- Likes per post
- Shares per post
- Comments per post
- Clicks per post

There are numerous tools, mostly paid, that can help you track these statistics, and Buffer itself has an excellent analytics package.

Beyond follower growth and engagement trends, the website Dashboard Junkie suggests six steps to measuring social media ROI:[34]

1. **Define conversion goals** — what do you want the visitor to do? Much of how you will structure your conversion goals depends on what you're selling. You're not going to sell an $800,000 tractor from one visit to your landing page, no matter how good your copy is. But you might get the user on your email list, after which you can invite them to a demo, which might get them much more interested.

2. **Track conversions with Google Analytics.** Use your *Thank You* page to track conversions as the only way to get to that page is via a completed purchase. Assign an average monetary value to each conversion type. Let's say you sell that $800,000 tractor. If you know how much you spent on customer acquisition, the process of attracting new customers, you can get a good idea how much the conversion is worth. Say you spent $10,000 on online advertising and you sold two tractors. Unless your margin is extremely low, that's a darned good ROI. Conversion rate benchmarks differ significantly across industries, so be sure you measure yourself against your industry standards. Here's what Google can tell you:

    - 100 people clicked on your link to visit your landing page.
    - 20 clicked through to buy.

- Only five actually completed the purchase. We know this because, you remember, the only way they get to the *Thank You* page is via the purchase page.

3. **Assign a dollar value to each conversion.** You may have a book for sale that's $12, and an online course that costs $200, so account for that in your calculation.

4. **Track incoming traffic.** Google Analytics is your friend, as you measure traffic to your *Thank You* page.

5. **Figure costs.** How much have you invested? This includes paid services, such as Buffer, Hootsuite, or social media monitoring services and staff time. How much did you make as a result of your efforts? Calculate the cost of any advertising you ran to drive traffic to your landing page, and any other costs associated with the campaign. Let's say you're selling a $10 widget. You've launched a campaign and are using content marketing to get leads and conversions. You're posting links to the landing page on your website that you've created specifically to sell this widget, and a *Thank You* page that the visitor will land on after the sale is complete. Measure your costs against the profits.

6. **Listen to the numbers.** You know from your analytics 100 people clicked on your link to visit your landing page and 20 of them clicked through to buy. Or maybe 20 people clicked through to the landing page, but only one made a purchase. Depending on what you're selling, this may not be too great. What does that tell you? Right, your landing page probably isn't as cool as

you think it is.

Measuring your results is essential to meeting your goals. Like your GPS, your analytics can guide you to the best copy, images, and sites for your content, both paid and organic.

No strategy will work if it's ill informed. Be armed with knowledge and understand of your audience and adjust your content delivery based on their responses. Always make decisions that are informed not by your own guesses and preferences, but by those of your audience.

Summary

Whew. We've covered a lot of material in these pages. We started with customer discovery, your website, blogging, content marketing, social media, and ended with email marketing and ROI. None of these are enough on their own. Like any good team, each has its own position and function.

Your website is the foundation of your online presence and establishes the tone for all of your communications, online and off. If your online presence is a wheel, your website is the hub, and social media, your blog, and email marketing are spokes that point back to the hub. Ideally, your blog shares the domain of your website, and new posts enrich the SEO of your site accordingly. All social media posts point to your blog unless they are curated content from another source. Your email marketing points back to your website via links or teasers for stories.

If you're fortunate enough to have a team, get together to plan your editorial calendar, and incorporate not just your blog, but social media and email so that everything works together. If you're solo, set aside plenty of time to think through each medium and how it fits into the greater picture. Don't miss an opportunity to promote yourself. Add links to your email signature, offer to speak at local conferences and meetings, and get involved in interest groups and user groups. If there are none in your area, start one. Combine your online presence with offline networking.

Prioritize

I'm guessing you don't have time to do everything we've talked about. You have a couple of choices.

- **Outsource.** There are plenty of freelance professionals who are equipped to take on what you can't. Be careful who you hire; you need someone who understands both your business and the online community. You may be tempted to try to save money. Don't. I shake my head when I hear a business say they hired a random college student to do social media or that they have delegated it to the intern. Consider what is at stake. We've talked about the consequences of social media blunders. You put your online reputation in the hands of the person you give your passwords to. Be sure it's someone who is up to the task.
- **Eliminate.** You don't necessarily have to be everywhere. Of course you need a website, and I strongly advise a

blog. If your resources are low, choose one social network that you know your audience frequents. Concentrate on that one and don't worry about the rest. Once you've built a following you can decide whether or not it's worth it to devote more time or outsource. Be realistic about your time constraints and resources. Earlier this year I stopped using Pinterest. While I may have audience members there, it's just not a place I like and feel comfortable. Though I check in on it now and again, I have given myself permission to (mostly) skip it.

There are no one-size-fits-all solutions in marketing, and even less so in online marketing. It's up to you to determine what works best, based on educated guesses about your audience.

My hope is that you feel more comfortable and equipped to manage your online presence on your own, or more able to hire intelligently if you determine it's not in your best interest to do it yourself.

References

1 http://www.cnbc.com/2014/01/15/the-five-year-anniversary-of-twitters-defining-moment.html

2 http://www.telegraph.co.uk/technology/twitter/4269765/New-York-plane-crash-Twitter-breaks-the-news-again.html

3 https://www.wordtracker.com/academy/keyword-research/guides/long-tail-keywords

4 https://marketingland.com/mobile-top-sites-165725'

5 https://www.codeinwp.com/blog/wordpress-statistics/

6 http://www.wptemplate.com/tutorials/safety-and-security-of-wordpress-blog-infographic.html

7 https://www.impactbnd.com/blogging-statistics-55-reasons-blogging-creates-55-more-traffic

8 https://www.linkedin.com/pulse/organic-traffic-why-important-krohn-online-traffic-generation/

9 http://www.techclient.com/blogging-statistics/

10 http://www.smartpassiveincome.com/tutorials/start-podcast-pats-complete-step-step-podcasting-tutorial/

11 11 https://www.impactbnd.com/blogging-statistics-55-reasons-blogging-creates-55-more-traffic

12 Deere & Company, "The History of John Deere," accessed April 6, 2013, http:// www. deere.com/ wps/ dcom/ en_US/ corporate/ our_company/ about_us/ history/ history. page.

13 http://www.pewresearch.org/data-trend/media-and-technology/social-networking-use/#

14 http://expandedramblings.com/index.php/snapchat-statistics/

15 http://www.pewinternet.org/fact-sheet/social-media/

16 http://learningenglish.voanews.com/a/facebook-has-more-users-than-china-population/2732122.html

17 https://blog.hubspot.com/blog/tabid/6307/bid/33800/Photos-on-Facebook-Generate-53-More-Likes-Than-the-Average-Post-NEW-DATA.aspx#sm.000emlf7p1d7zf6jsvl2g-0m5lbje3

18 https://blog.bufferapp.com/3rd-party-facebook

19 http://expandedramblings.com/index.php/important-instagram-stats/

20 blogs.forrester.com/nate_elliott/14-04-29-instagram_is_the_king_of_social_engagement

21 http://www.cmo.com/articles/2014/3/10/mind_blowing_stats_SlideShare.html

22 http://expandedramblings.com/index.php/youtube-statistics

23 https://www.roadsidedentalmarketing.com/blog/second-largest-search-engine/

24 http://expandedramblings.com/index.php/vimeo-statistics/

25 https://www.ftc.gov/tips-advice/business-center/guidance/can-spam-act-compliance-guide-business

26 https://blog.hubspot.com/marketing/plain-text-vs-html-emails-data#sm.0000jqvx-tyr9dd8lxzx100axjbm5t

27 http://marketingland.com/majority-emails-opened-apple-devices-android-users-pay-attention-115945) cites a report from MovableInk (https://movableink.com/

28 https://www.marketingsherpa.com/article/chart/personal-subject-lines

29 https://mailchimp.com/resources/research/effects-of-list-segmentation-on-email-marketing-stats/

30 https://blog.hubspot.com/marketing/7-effective-lead-nurturing-tactics#sm.0000jqvx-tyr9dd8lxzx100axjbm5t

31 https://blog.hubspot.com/marketing/7-effective-lead-nurturing-tactics#sm.0000jqvx-tyr9dd8lxzx100axjbm5t

32 http://www.lenskold.com/content/landing_2013_B2b_Lead_Generation_Marketing_ROI

33 https://blog.bufferapp.com/measure-social-media-engagement

34 http://www.dashboardjunkie.com/measure-online-roi-six-simple-steps

Index

T

CPSIA information can be obtained
at www.ICGtesting.com
Printed in the USA
BVOW08s1035010218
506903BV00016B/165/P